What Others Are Saying About *It's All About Jesus*

Charlie Tremendous and Ken Blanchard are two of the best and most outwardly focused human beings I have ever known. They are both great friends and deeply rooted in Christ. What a treasure to have this collection of readings.

—Bob Buford
Founder, Leadership Network
Author, *Halftime* and *Finishing Well*

I have never known anyone who loved Jesus more than Charlie. His life and this book truly epitomizes *It's All About Jesus*. You will be blessed as I have been.

—Ron Glosser
Retired CEO, Hershey Trust
and the M.S. Hershey Foundation

From the moment we are born we are all on a journey. Many of us follow maps, some of our own making and others of religion, doctrine and culture pointing to our destination. But beyond all such mapping lies our true destination. "It's All About Jesus."

—James H. Amos, Jr.
CEO, Tasti D-Lite,
Chairman Emeritus, Mail Boxes Etc.

It's All About Jesus is a brilliantly written book chock-full of inspiration and encouragement for those who want to live a Christ-filled life. Moreover, it's a joy to read. There are hymns to be hummed; prayers to recite; and Scripture to contemplate...and then there are the *lists*. For people who enjoy reading and writing lists as I do, this book just might provide a little slice of heaven here on earth. I'm particularly fond of the lists titled, "The Blood of Jesus 'A' to 'Z'" and the "Titles of Jesus." Each listed item has a corresponding Biblical reference that makes it a handy companion when reading the Good Book. Compiled by three of the most Christ-centered guys I know, *It's All About Jesus* is sure to find a permanent place on your bedside table. Although I'm certain he is here in spirit, I wish Charlie "Tremendous" Jones would witness the launch of this gem of a book. No doubt he would have dismissed such praise, saying: "It's not about me, it's all about Jesus!"

—Paul J. Meyer
Founder of Success Motivation International, Inc., and forty-plus other companies; *New York Times* bestselling author

It's All About JESUS

Ken Blanchard
Charlie "Tremendous" Jones
Bob Phillips

It's All About Jesus

Published by
Tremendous Life Books
206 West Allen Street
Mechanicsburg, PA 17055

Book Production Services Provided by Gregory A. Dixon

ISBN: 978-1-933715-83-4

Printed in the United States of America

Dedicated to the glory of God
and the lifting up of His Son

Jesus

Contents

Part III: All Roads Lead to Jesus: How That Can Be True for You

Part IV: Learning More About Jesus

Part V: Books Will Help You Grow in Character

In Remembrance
Charlie "Tremendous" Jones
October 23, 1927—October 16, 2008

For a number of years Charlie wanted to produce a book that had a central focus on Jesus. It was his driving passion. ***It's All About Jesus*** was begun while he was living through his battle with cancer. Although he was unable to see the final book in print, he did see most of the material and directed the concepts.

It has been said that you can tell the size of a ship by the wake it leaves behind. Charlie's wake is enormous. His influence has touched the lives of thousands and thousands of people through his motivational speaking, writing, and tape recordings. He was an avid reader, a humanitarian, and a beloved father and grandfather. Charlie would just say he was a "follower of Jesus."

Charlie's positive spirit was contagious. He attempted to encourage and say something kind to everyone he met. His nickname was 'Tremendous Jones.' This was given to him because he was always saying "Tremendous."

"How are you Charlie?"
"Tremendous!"
What kind of day has it been Charlie?"
"Tremendous!"
"What do you think the future will be like Charlie?"
"Tremendous!"

Charlie will be loved and remembered for many of his sayings. Probably one of the most familiar is, "You will be the same five years from now as you are today except for the people you meet and the books you read." Charlie loved books and passed on this excitement for reading at every chance he got. It was the foundation for starting his company, Executive Books.

We would encourage you to check out the many wonderful books offered through this service by going to their website at www.TremendousLifeBooks.com

During Charlie's last days, many friends stopped by to express their love and concern for him. Even while he was in the process of dying he had a plan to get people to read. Well wishers would ask, "Is there anything I can do for you, Charlie?" He would reply, "Yes. Could you read the Bible to me?" Sometimes he would choose a devotional book for them to read. All of the reading by friends had a purpose. Charlie wanted those readers to hear the great truths from the Bible or positive thoughts from the books. He wanted the readers to get encouragement from what they were reading more than to support him. Charlie attempted to continue to reach out and help others in the midst of his own physical suffering.

Charlie's life is an example of how one person can be a shining light in the midst of a darkened world. His light helped to challenge and light the lives of many others who wish to follow his example. Charlie "Tremendous" Jones will be sorely missed. However, we can keep his memory alive as we influence others. Charlie used to say, "You only keep what you give away." Charlie must have had a great deal of emotional and spiritual wealth because he gave so much away.

Charlie would often summarize his life story by saying:

"I'm not what I think I am,
I'm not what I hoped I'd be,
I'm not what I ought to be,
But by the grace of God,
I'm not what I was.
I once was lost, but now I'm found,
Was blind but now I see."

It's All About Jesus

Charlie also had a favorite prayer. It went like this:

> *"Dear Lord, if I can be of most use by being of no use, then let me be learning to be of no use—if that's the way I can be of most use. But please, Lord, never let my usefulness be the basis of my joy. Let my joy always be His joy, Himself, Christ in me . . . plus nothing."*

To Charlie, Jesus was more than enough. He would often say, "Jesus is better than His blessings, His gifts, His feelings, and His healing. He is all of these. Jesus is everything."

It would be wonderful if we could ask Charlie one more question.

"Charlie, what is it like to be in Heaven with Jesus?"

We know what his answer would be.

"It's more than TREMENDOUS!"

Ken Blanchard
Bob Phillips

A Word from the Authors

> *If you wish to be miserable, think about yourself; about what you want, what you like, what respect people ought to pay you, what people think of you; and then to you nothing will be pure. You will spoil everything you touch; you will make sin and misery for yourself out of everything God sends you; you will be as wretched as you choose.*
>
> Charles Kingsley

In 1969, Frank Sinatra popularized a song written by Paul Anka . . . the title was *My Way*. The lyrics talk about an older man reviewing the course of his life. He mentions his regrets, his tough times, his laughter and tears, and his determination to survive. At the end of each refrain, and at the closing of the song, he basically says, "I did it my way."

Actually, that phrase, "I did it my way," is not a surprising comment. We think it could be the statement of everyone who has ever lived. From the cradle to the grave we all have a tendency to be more concerned for our own well being than for the well being of others.

Babies aren't concerned about their parent's lack of sleep or their busy schedules. When they are hungry, hurt, or they need to be changed, they let the whole world know of their discontent. They will persist with a loud voice until their personal needs are met.

But it doesn't stop there. Have you ever been to a store when a toddler or a younger child throws a temper tantrum? They don't care who's watching or if their parents get embarrassed. They want what they want when they want it.

So, what else is new? This type of behavior can be seen in every culture and country of the world. How the parents deal with that behavior varies but the tantrums have a universal language.

Teenagers are no exception to the rule. They become unhappy when they don't get to wear what their friends are wearing or go where their friends are going. They can make life uncomfortable in the home when they don't get their way. They can pout, slam doors, turn to drugs, and on occasion run away.

There are some situations when we can smile at a child's temper tantrum. Their behavior is so obvious, predictable, and sometimes humorous. But just imagine that child growing up and continuing to have temper tantrums as an adult. At this point the behavior ceases to be amusing and can be quite destructive. They can be seen threatening people who innocently cut them off while driving on the highway. They can yell and scream at their family at home. They can pound tables, put their fist through the door, and sometimes become verbally or physically abusive to the closest members of their family.

We are all basically selfish, self-centered, and self-absorbed. When "King Me" is on the throne, everyone needs to watch out. Did you hear about the selfish young man who was eating dinner with some friends? Towards the end of the meal, a platter of chocolate cake was brought to the table and placed next to him. He noticed that one piece of cake was much larger than all of the rest. He determined that he wanted that large piece for himself. However, he was not finished eating what was on his plate. He started to chew as fast as he could with the hope that no one would ask for the platter of cake to be passed. But he didn't make it. Someone said, "Would you please pass the chocolate cake?"

The young man was in a dilemma. To insure that he got the largest piece of cake, he took his thumb and pushed it into the special piece and said, "This is my piece of cake!" Everyone looked a little shocked.

The Bible suggests that whatsoever a man sows, that he will also reap. So as the platter was passed around the table, everyone took their thumb and jammed it into the large piece of cake saying, "This is his piece of cake! This is his piece of cake! This is his piece of cake!" So much for dealing with selfishness.

The topic of *self* is very popular. If you go to the World Wide Web and punch in the word *self* you may be surprised to find 37,600,000 sites that address the topic in some form or another. There are 474,000 sites for *self-esteem*, 198,000 sites for *self-confidence*, and 180,000 sites for *self-image*.

The focus on self has become very popular during the past few decades. Just go to the self-help section of your bookstore or library and see how many books are written on the topic.

The coin of self-esteem has two sides . . . one can be Positive, Practical, and Productive; and the other can be Damaging, Detrimental, and Dangerous. For example, self-analysis can be good if it helps us to determine our abilities, establish an action plan for growth, or have an honest appraisal of our talent and skills. On the other hand, self-analysis can lead us to negatively compare ourselves with others. We do not all look like movie stars or top models. We do not all have the ability to be a top Olympic athlete or sports figure. We are not all brilliant students or talented musicians. We are not all wealthy and live in mansions, and vacation on yachts or on the Riviera. Comparison with others drives many people to develop a poor self-image and negative self-esteem.

Most people will admit that self-pity, self-doubt, and self-conceit are not healthy or beneficial. There are, however, traits of self that the majority of people view as positive and constructive such as self-control, self-reliance, and self-sacrifice.

We would like to suggest that there is something even more beneficial, healthy, and powerful than focusing on self: It is learning to look to Jesus.

On one occasion the disciples of John the Baptist came to

him with a concern that people were beginning to follow Jesus rather than him. John had shared with his disciples that Jesus was the Messiah but they did not fully understand. They were upset that Jesus was getting more attention than John.

John replied,

> *"God in heaven appoints each person's work. You yourselves know how plainly I told you that I am not the Messiah. I am here to prepare the way for him—that is all. The bride will go where the bridegroom is. A bridegroom's friend rejoices with him. I am the bridegroom's friend, and I am filled with joy at his success. He must become greater and greater, and I must become less and less."*

That's the motivation for this book and the desire of our hearts: that we all may begin to turn from the focus on self to a focus on Jesus. May we join Paul in saying, "For to me, to live is Christ, and to die is gain . . . according to my earnest expectation and hope that in nothing I shall be ashamed, but with all boldness, as always, so now also Christ will be magnified in my body, whether by life or by death." And may we say with Jesus himself, "and I, if I be lifted up from the earth, will draw all men unto me."

Ken Blanchard
Charlie Jones
Bob Phillips

A Comment about Writing Style

The writing of this book was a joint effort of three friends who have spent many years speaking, teaching, and consulting with various businesses and organizations. We could have chosen to write it entirely in the third person, thus keeping our personalities out of the material and illustrations. We could have chosen to split up the content, with each of us writing certain chapters.

For the most part, we decided to write the illustrations in the first person and much of the text in third person. Except for sharing our own journeys of grace and Ken's reflections on Jesus as a leader, by changing the names of the people or situations in the illustrations . . . and not identifying who is speaking . . . we have kept the power of the event while protecting the confidentiality of the individuals.

We felt that a first-person account of a real-life event would be a more dynamic form of presentation. It is our hope that this style of writing will keep the flow of thought running smoothly and the reader will sense the reality of a true-life incident. You, as the reader, may be more comfortable pretending either Ken, Charlie, or Bob is the only author. If that would be helpful, then please proceed with that concept in mind. We are all in agreement with the thoughts presented and speak with a unified mind.

Part I
It's All About Jesus

Through Jesus,
We Can Experience a Life
That is Exciting and Fulfilling

It's All About Jesus

It has been said that there are seven major sins. They are wealth without works, pleasure without conscience, knowledge without character, commerce without morality, science without humanity, worship without sacrifice, and politics without principle. Much of society seems to focus on what is called the "Cafeteria Plan"—self service only. Listed below are self words that can be destructive.

Damaging, Detrimental, Dangerous

Self-Absorbed
Self-Abuse
Self-Complacent
Self-Conceit
Self-Conscious
Self-Despair
Self-Important
Self-Interest

The focus on self is not all entirely bad from a human standpoint. It is healthy to have a realistic self-image. It is also good to have a certain amount of self-reliance and to be a self-starter when it comes to work. Society benefits greatly by individuals who are self-sacrificing and are willing to face danger. This was exemplified by the firefighters and police in the World Trade Center bombing on 9/ll . . . and by military personnel who go to war to protect our nation.

Listed below are self words that are beneficial.

Positive, Practical, Productive

Self-Analysis
Self-Confident
Self-Control
Self-Defense
Self-Denial
Self-Discipline

Self-Forgiveness
Self-Knowledge

As good and helpful as the above self words may be there is a better or higher attainment to seek. It is to focus on Jesus who is the author and finisher of our faith. By concentrating on Him we can experience a life that is exciting and fulfilling.

Listed below are words that help to take us to a higher plane.

DYNAMIC, LIFEGIVING, MATCHLESS

Christ-Examined
Christ-Reliant
Christ-Controlled
Christ-Protected
Christ-Likeness
Christ-Empowered
Christ-Forgiven
Christ-Awareness

Read Demosthenes or Cicero; read Plato, Aristotle, or any others of that class; I grant you that you will be attracted, delighted, moved, enraptured by them in a surprising manner; but if, after reading them, you turn to the perusal of the sacred volume, whether you are willing or unwilling, it will affect you so powerfully, it will so penetrate your heart, and impress itself so strangely on your mind that, compared with its energetic influence, the beauties of rhetoricians and philosophers will almost entirely disappear; so that it is easy to perceive something divine in the sacred Scriptures, which far surpasses the highest attainments and ornaments of human industry.

John Calvin
from *Institutes of the Christian Religion*, 1536

Christ-Examined

To be Self-Absorbed is damaging, detrimental, and dangerous. Samuel Johnson said, “He that considers how little he dwells upon the condition of others will learn how little the attention of others is attracted by himself.”

The Bible suggests, “Arrogance will bring your downfall, but if you are humble, you will be respected” (Proverbs 29:23).

Self-Analysis can be positive, practical, and productive. W. Clement Stone suggested that, “There is little difference in people . . . the little difference is attitude. The big difference is whether it is positive or negative.”

There are two things that most people don’t want to be accused of . . . the first is that they don’t have a sense of humor. The second is that they are pessimistic. Everyone prefers to see themselves as optimistic and having a healthy sense of humor. However, the truth is that we all know people who are pessimistic and have no humor in their lives. You see, sometimes there is a big discrepancy between how people see themselves and how they actually behave.

Self-analysis is not always an easy task. On one extreme when we compare our talents and skills to other people it is easy to find those who excel far above us. As we compare ourselves to those high performers we can become discouraged and disheartened. On the other extreme we can find individuals who are real losers in our opinion. As we compare ourselves to their failings we can become arrogant, proud, and conceited. We can arrive at the conclusion that we are better than we actually are. However, people may disagree with our viewpoint. You see, we all have a tendency to judge ourselves by our motives and judge other people by their actions.

To analyze something is to break it down into smaller parts and look at those individual parts carefully, honestly, and fully. There are those things that everyone does well and those that could be improved upon . . . and each person has their own uniqueness. Some people are great communicators and talk easily to strangers. Others have to put forth a great deal of energy in this area. There are those who excel in math and science and those who don't. Certain individuals do well as doctors and surgeons and there are people who can't stand the sight of blood and would faint at the prospect of being stuck with a hypodermic needle.

It is very beneficial to have a good wholesome understanding of what we like to do and are good at. It is also healthy to have a balanced view of those things we could develop or improve upon in our lives. Countless books have been written on self-improvement and establishing a positive attitude.

To be Christ-examined is dynamic, matchless, and life giving. Although self-analysis has its benefits and its drawbacks there is another aspect of analysis that has far reaching ramifications. It is the examination, analysis, or comparison of our lives with the ideals of the Bible. There is no more important analysis than God's view of how we are doing.

For example, in the third chapter of Colossians God suggests a standard by which we can evaluate ourselves. He suggests that we put to death our earthly nature which gets involved with "sexual immorality, impurity, lust, evil desires, and greed, which is idolatry."

How are you doing? Has the Internet been a struggle for you?

He goes on to say that we should get rid of "anger, rage, malice, slander, and filthy language. And do not lie to each other."

How are you doing? When was the last time you got angry . . . and with whom? Did it produce a positive result?

He then tells us to fill our lives with "compassion, kindness, humility, gentleness, and patience." He tells us to "bear with each other and forgive whatever grievances you may have against another."

It's All About Jesus

How are you doing? Have you been patient with your family? Do you need to forgive someone?

As a climax in the analysis of our spiritual life God says that "whatever you do, whether in word or deed, do it all in the name of the Lord Jesus, giving thanks to God the Father through him."

How are you doing? Has your focus been on how you can please the Lord by the things that come out of your mouth and the deeds you do for others?

God wants to help us improve our relationships and He wants to help curb the old nature that loves to go its own selfish way.

How are you doing?

> *For by the grace given me I say to every one of you: Do not think of yourself more highly than you ought, but rather think of yourself with sober judgment, in accordance with the measure of faith God has given you. Just as each of us has one body with many members, and these members do not all have the same function, so in Christ we who are many form one body, and each member belongs to all the others. We have different gifts, according to the grace given us. If a man's gift is prophesying, let him use it in proportion to his faith. If it is serving, let him serve; if it is teaching, let him teach; if it is encouraging, let him encourage; if it is contributing to the needs of others, let him give generously; if it is leadership, let him govern diligently; if it is showing mercy, let him do it cheerfully.*
>
> Romans 12:3-8

It's All About Jesus

Test me, O LORD, and try me, examine my heart and my mind; for your love is ever before me.

Psalm 26:2-3

I the LORD search the heart and examine the mind, to reward a man according to his conduct, according to what his deeds deserve.

Jeremiah 17:10

Examine yourselves to see whether you are in the faith; test yourselves. Do you not realize that Christ Jesus is in you–unless, of course, you fail the test?

2 Corinthians 13:5

Wonderful Grace of Jesus

Wonderful grace of Jesus,
Greater than all my sin;
How shall my tongue describe it,
Where shall its praise begin?
Taking away my burden,
Setting my spirit free,
For the wonderful grace of Jesus reaches me.

Wonderful the matchless grace of Jesus,
Deeper than the mighty rolling sea;
Higher than the mountain, sparkling like a fountain,
All sufficient grace for even me;
Broader than the scope of my transgressions,
Greater far than all my sin and shame;
O magnify the precious name of Jesus,
Praise His name!

Wonderful grace of Jesus,
Reaching to all the lost,
By it I have been pardoned,
Saved to the uttermost;
Chains have been torn asunder,
Giving me liberty,
For the wonderful grace of Jesus reaches me.

Wonderful grace of Jesus,
Reaching the most defiled,
By its transforming power
Making me God's dear child,
Purchasing peace and heaven
For all eternity—
And the wonderful grace of Jesus reaches me.

Hymn by Haldor Lillenas, 1918

Christ-Reliant

To be involved with Self-Abuse is damaging, detrimental, and dangerous. No one likes to be around people who are constantly putting themselves down. If the person keeps telling others that they are no good, not capable, and unworthy . . . pretty soon they will be believed. This gives rise to the statement, "He is a self-made man, which shows what happens when you don't follow the directions." The Bible suggests that, "A happy heart makes the face cheerful, but heartache crushes the spirit" (Proverbs 15:13).

Being Self-Confident can be positive, practical, and productive. Theodore Roosevelt addressed this subject when he said, "Whenever you are asked if you can do a job, tell 'em certainly, I can!—and get busy and find out how to do it."

The police and military often refer to certain individuals by saying that they have "command presence." This term is used to describe people who seem to have a certain leadership quality that draws people to them. Not only are people attracted to their demeanor but they also willingly follow this person.

Command presence is immediately sensed but is sometimes hard to describe because it involves a number of different qualities. They include such things as content of words, tone of voice, and nonverbal actions.

Two people could say the same thing to a group and each get a different response. One person speaks with confidence and strength of conviction. The other does not. One stands erect and stately and the other slouches with inferiority. One looks the people in the eye and the other looks down or away from their gaze. One gestures with enthusiasm and the other stands like a stick in the mud. Which person would you have a tendency to follow?

Having self-confidence is usually an attractive quality especially if arrogance has been replaced by humility. Some people think that humility is a sign of weakness. Nothing could be further from the truth. In fact, Ken and Norman Vincent Peale, in their book *The Power of Ethical Management*, contend that ***people with humility don't think less of themselves, they just think about themselves less***.

Humility is a choice to be of service to others and to not demand rights, promote a position, or exercise power over others . . . even though a person could do that if they desired to. It takes great strength of character to put others ahead of you.

Self-confidence comes from doing your homework about your field of interest, your values, or your moral convictions. The person who knows what they believe and why they believe it is a rare commodity in today's culture. Too many people would rather not state what they believe for fear of being criticized or rejected by others.

Have you done your homework about what you believe about:

How to get along in marriage . . .
How to raise children . . .
How to handle finances . . .
How to get along with people . . .
How to develop friendships . . .
How to give yourself in service . . .

Are you confident about what you believe about:

God . . .
Jesus Christ . . .
The Holy Spirit . . .
The importance of prayer . . .
The need for Bible study . . .
The necessity of the church . . .
The importance of sharing
your faith with others . . .

To be Christ-Reliant is dynamic, matchless, and life giving.

It's All About Jesus

One of the most influential people the world has ever known was the Apostle Paul. Before his encounter with Jesus he did not suffer from low self-esteem or lack of confidence in his abilities. The Apostle Paul was a man who radiated self-confidence. This can be seen when he said in the third chapter of Philippians:

> *Yet I could have confidence in myself if anyone could. If others have reason for confidence in their own efforts, I have even more! For I was circumcised when I was eight days old, having been born into a pure-blooded Jewish family that is a branch of the tribe of Benjamin. So I am a real Jew if there ever was one! What's more, I was a member of the Pharisees, who demand the strictest obedience to the Jewish law. And zealous? Yes, in fact, I harshly persecuted the church. And I obeyed the Jewish law so carefully that I was never accused of any fault.*

But Paul does not stop there. He takes an honest and insightful look at his own accomplishments and says:

> *I once thought all these things were so very important, but now I consider them worthless because of what Christ has done. Yes, everything else is worthless when compared with the priceless gain of knowing Christ Jesus my Lord. I have discarded everything else, counting it all as garbage, so that I may have Christ and become one with him. I no longer count on my own goodness or my ability to obey God's law, but I trust Christ to save me. For God's way of making us right with himself depends on faith. As a result, I can really know Christ and experience the mighty power that raised him from the dead. I can learn what it means to suffer with him, sharing in his death, so that, somehow, I*

can experience the resurrection from the dead!

Paul goes on to clarify that he is not perfect or better than other people. He just simply shares his desire and goal to change his focus from self to Jesus and encourages us to do the same. Even though Paul had confidence he realized that it did not hold a candle to the importance of his relationship with Jesus. He goes on to say:

> *I don't mean to say that I have already achieved these things or that I have already reached perfection! But I keep working toward that day when I will finally be all that Christ Jesus saved me for and wants me to be. No, dear brothers and sisters, I am still not all I should be, but I am focusing all my energies on this one thing: Forgetting the past and looking forward to what lies ahead, I strain to reach the end of the race and receive the prize for which God, through Christ Jesus, is calling us up to heaven. I hope all of you who are mature Christians will agree on these things. If you disagree on some point, I believe God will make it plain to you. But we must be sure to obey the truth we have learned already.*

There comes a day in all of our lives when our confidence runs out of gas. It is a time when we realize that we don't have any answers for the problems facing us. They may be relationship difficulties, financial disaster, emotional depression, health disruption, or job related dilemmas. Each of us will face a time when we are at the end of our rope. It is at the time when we realize that we can't do it alone, that we need to have confidence not in ourselves, but in God who is our strength.

> *In you, O LORD, I have taken refuge; let me never be put to shame. Rescue me and deliver me in your righteousness; turn your ear to me*

and save me. Be my rock of refuge, to which I can always go; give the command to save me, for you are my rock and my fortress. Deliver me, O my God, from the hand of the wicked, from the grasp of evil and cruel men. For you have been my hope, O Sovereign LORD, my confidence since my youth. From birth I have relied on you; you brought me forth from my mother's womb. I will ever praise you. I have become like a portent [a calamity about to occur] to many, but you are my strong refuge. My mouth is filled with your praise, declaring your splendor all day long. Do not cast me away when I am old; do not forsake me when my strength is gone.

Psalm 71:1-9

I am still confident of this: I will see the goodness of the LORD in the land of the living. Wait for the LORD; be strong and take heart and wait for the LORD.

Psalm 27:13-14 NIV

I thank my God every time I remember you. In all my prayers for all of you, I always pray with joy because of your partnership in the gospel from the first day until now, being confident of this, that he who began a good work in you will carry it on to completion until the day of Christ Jesus.

Philippians 1:3-6 NIV

Alas! And Did My Savior Bleed?

Alas! And did my Savior bleed
And did my Sovereign die?
Would He devote that sacred head
For sinners such as I?

Was it for sins that I have done
He suffered on the tree?
Amazing pity! Grace unknown!
And love beyond degree!

Well might the sun in darkness hide
And shut His glories in,
When Christ, the great Redeemer, died
For man the creature's sin.

Thus might I hide my blushing face
While His dear cross appears,
Dissolve my heart in thankfulness,
And melt mine eyes to tears.

But drops of grief can ne'er repay
The debt of love I owe;
Here, Lord, I give myself away—
'Tis all that I can do.

Hymn by Isaac Watts, 1707

Christ-Controlled

Being Self-Complacent can be damaging, detrimental, and dangerous. It has been said that self-satisfied people are very pleased with their own thoughts, words, and behaviors. The great preacher Henry Ward Beecher said, "The prouder a man is, the more he thinks he deserves; and the more he thinks he deserves, the less he really does deserve." The Bible says that, "The Lord detests all the proud of heart. Be sure of this: They will not go unpunished" (Proverbs 16:5).

Learning to have Self-Control is positive, practical, and productive.

It has been said that someone is strong who conquers others; those who conquer themselves are mighty. Sir Winston Churchill suggests that a person with self-control should "Never give in, never give in, never, never, never, never—in nothing, great or small, large or petty—never give in except to convictions of honor and good sense."

Carl, a friend of mine, described a recurring nightmare that had become an obsession.

"I run as fast as I can, yet it feels as if everything around me is in slow motion. I try to yell but no sound comes. I can feel the panic as the beast draws closer and closer. I know that this time my life will end.

"That dream has bothered me for years," he continued. "But recently, something far worse has taken its place. This new monster is larger and ten times scarier than the beast of my nightmares. Not only do I battle it during the night, I now struggle with it during the day."

I could see the agitation in Carl's face as he sat forward in his chair. "You see, it all started about a month ago when I brought home the new computer. I had hooked up with an Internet service provider and was surfing the web when something popped on the screen. Out of curiosity, I clicked on the advertisement, and up came a pornography site. I thought to myself, *I've heard about these sites. I wonder what all the fuss is about?* At first, I only looked at a few pictures and then shut it down. I knew this was not the best thing for me to be doing. When I went to bed that night I could not get those pictures out of my mind."

Carl leaned back in the chair and gazed out the window for a moment. The silence seemed to last a long time. As he turned back, I could hear the anguish in his voice. "I'm hooked. I know that I'm addicted. I can't stop looking at those pictures. It's a monster I can't get away from. I think about it all day long at work. *How can I kill this beast?*"

Like Carl, we all deal with some negative thoughts, emotions, or behaviors that seem to overpower and control our lives. Can you identify with any of the 'monsters' on the list below?

Fear	Hair twisting	Nail biting
Worry	Depression	Passing gas
Anxiety	Forgetfulness	Sloppiness
Anger	Fidgeting	Obsessions
Resentment	Knuckle cracking	Hatred
Unforgiveness	Overeating	Toe tapping
Bitterness	Being late	Belching
Hatred	Guilt	Gum snapping

It is quite easy for thoughts, emotions, and behaviors to become habits. It has been said that habits are at first cobwebs and then they soon become cables.

To be able to exercise self-control in any of the above is a wonderful thing; however, it is not as easy as one might think.

Sometimes it is quite difficult to deny yourself a favorite dessert, or to be on time, or to get rid of some negative thought.

Do you remember seeing a small child's toy that had a number of colored pegs on a board? The object of the toy was to take a small wooden hammer and hit the pegs until they went flat with the board. Then you would turn the toy over and hit the pegs in the opposite direction. You could do this all day long but the pegs would not come out of the holes. That is the way with habits. They are hard to get out of our lives.

The only way to get pegs out of the child's toy is to drive out a peg with a different peg. The new peg drives out the old peg. The only way to get rid of some negative thought or habit is to drive it out with a *positive* thought or habit.

Becoming Christ-Controlled is dynamic, matchless, and life-giving.

"For the LORD sees clearly what a man does, examining every path he takes. An evil man is held captive by his own sins; they are ropes that catch and hold him. He will die for lack of self-control; he will be lost because of his incredible folly" (Proverbs 5:21-23).

"But you, man of God, flee from all this, and pursue righteousness, godliness, faith, love, endurance and gentleness. Fight the good fight of the faith. Take hold of the eternal life to which you were called when you made your good confession in the presence of many witnesses" (1 Timothy 6:11-12).

Psychologists estimate that the average person has approximately 50,000 thoughts enter and leave his or her mind every day. *(No wonder I'm so tired!)* Although we cannot always choose which thoughts enter our minds, we do decide whether we entertain them or not. The great reformer Martin Luther expressed this concept when he spoke of troublesome thoughts.

"We cannot stop the birds from flying over our heads, but we can stop them from building a nest in our hair."

When we assume responsibility for our thinking, we assume responsibility for our feelings. The quality of our mental health is related directly to our thinking pattern.

For example, try to remember a painful experience out of your childhood. You may have been hurt by something a friend said. You might have been embarrassed in front of a group of your peers. Or it may have been the way you were treated by a parent.

I'll bet if you thought about this event long enough you could even feel the same emotions you felt when it occurred. If you continued thinking about the hurt, pain, and loss . . . those feelings would begin to grow. With enough focus and thought, you might even *increase* the suffering you felt. Do you see how you could be responsible for much of your own suffering by dwelling on it?

I do understand that some suffering is unjustly given and not fair. But you still have to choose how you respond to the unfairness. This is *elected* suffering. The only place that painful event is now taking place is in your mind. It is not presently real. It is in truth a past experience.

Now, imagine you are walking in a wooded forest when all of a sudden you hear a noise behind you. Instinctively you turn toward the sound. There, in the grass behind you, is a large snake that is about five feet long. You can tell it has been stalking you. Your turning around causes the snake to coil and shake its rattle. You can't move. You're especially fascinated by the sight of the snake because of its color. You have never seen anything like it before. It is sky blue with yellow stripes every four or five inches.

You step forward to look at this strange creature. Then it happens. Not the strike you were expecting, but something more frightening than that. You could not believe your eyes with the speed the snake moved. It simply disappeared . . . .

Do you know why it disappeared? Because I stopped writing about it. I stopped creating a word picture in your mind. The snake was not real. But even more than that, let me call your attention to the fact that while you were focusing on the blue-and-yellow snake, you were not thinking about your painful childhood experience.

The human mind can only entertain one thought at a time. Granted, it can shift thoughts rapidly, but we can only focus on one thought at a given moment. As you followed my promptings, you changed your thought process. The same principle can be applied to your emotions or behavior if you desire to control them. Remember, the choice is yours.

You might think, *That's just the power of positive thinking*. To which I would respond, "You're correct. It is." Where do you think this power of positive thinking came from? It comes from the Bible.

On one occasion, the apostle Paul was incarcerated in prison in Rome. He had been in prison before, and it was not much fun. While locked up he penned these words.

> *Always be full of joy in the Lord; I say it again, rejoice! Let everyone see that you are unselfish and considerate in all you do. Remember that the Lord is coming soon. Don't worry about anything; instead, pray about everything; tell God your needs, and don't forget to thank him for his answers. If you do this, you will experience God's peace, which is far more wonderful than the human mind can understand. His peace will keep your thoughts and hearts quiet and at rest as you trust in Christ Jesus.*
>
> *And now, brothers, as I close this letter, let me say this one more thing: Fix your thoughts on what is true and good and right. Think about*

> *things that are pure and lovely, and dwell on the fine, good things in others. Think about all you can praise God for and be glad about. Keep putting into practice all you learned from me and saw me doing, and the God of peace will be with you.*
>
> Philippians 4:4-9

Sure, we cannot change everything by thinking positive thoughts. I can't change the fact that my daughters and wife all suffered through difficult medical conditions. I cannot erase the head-on collision that almost took my life. These are *imposed* events that we had no control over. But we do have control over whether we become angry, resentful, or unforgiving. We must keep in mind the difference between *imposed* suffering and *elected* suffering.

When was the last time you asked Jesus to help take control of your negative thoughts, emotions, or behaviors? Today might be a good time to start.

This is the key to living a joyful life, even in the midst of hardship and pain. Remember, it's all about Jesus. He's the one who gives us that ability to forgive and experience His peace.

I Love to Tell the Story

I love to tell the story of unseen things above,
Of Jesus and His glory, of Jesus and His love;
I love to tell the story because I know 'tis true,
It satisfies my longings as nothing else can do.

I love to tell the story!
'Twill be my theme in glory—
To tell the old, old story
Of Jesus and His love.

I love to tell the story—'tis pleasant to repeat
What seems, each time I tell it, more wonderfully sweet;
I love to tell the story, for some have never heard
The message of salvation from God's own holy Word.

I love to tell the story, for those who know it best
Seem hungering and thirsting to hear it like the rest;
And when in scenes of glory I sing the new, new song,
'Twill be the old, old story that I have loved so long.

Hymn by Arabella Catherine Hankey, 1866

Christ-Protected

There is no question that Self-Conceit is damaging, detrimental, and dangerous. To be filled with a prideful, self-flattering, and egotistical view of oneself and your accomplishments can be harmful to most interpersonal relationships. Bruce Barton commented that "People who constantly brag are very boring." Someone else said, "Conceit is God's gift to little men." The Bible suggests, *"Do nothing out of selfish ambition or vain conceit, but in humility consider others better than yourselves"* (Philippians 2:3 NIV).

Sometimes Self-Defense can be positive, practical, and productive.

A number of years ago I went with my oldest daughter on a school field trip. I was helping to assist the teacher in herding excited grade-schoolers into a large yellow bus. We were going to visit a planetarium quite a distance from our city.

On the way back from visiting the planetarium we stopped for lunch at a McDonald's restaurant. My daughter and I happened to be the last ones off the bus. The teacher and the rest of the children had already entered the building.

I had my arm around her shoulder and we were casually talking about the field trip. All of a sudden I heard screeching tires in the almost empty parking lot and quickly looked up. In a split second I saw a car racing toward us driven by some laughing teenagers. There was no doubt that they were heading straight for us on purpose.

The next event only took micro-seconds. I pushed my daughter from my right side to the left so she would not be hit by the car. I turned and planted my left foot and kicked the door of the car with my right foot as it came by. We had just been assaulted with a 3,000 pound deadly weapon.

My reaction was defensive and quick. I felt the metal on the door give way under my foot. The driver slammed on his brakes and the two front doors flew open. I knew a fight was about to occur. I ran towards the driver's side of the car with the full intent of defending my daughter and myself. The driver barely got the car in gear before I reached him. He and those with him were yelling swear words as they drove off.

There are times in life when self-defense is right and justified. Occasionally we must rise to the occasion to protect our family, our possessions, or those who are defenseless. It may be in the form of physical, verbal, or written defense.

On one occasion, in the book of Philippians, the Apostle Paul had to defend his position as an Apostle by reminding the people that he was a Jew from the tribe of Benjamin, a zealous Pharisee. In the book of Acts he defended himself by attesting to his Roman citizenship for protection against false imprisonment.

Becoming Christ-Protected is dynamic, matchless, and life-giving.

However, there are also times where we do not defend ourselves at all. In those occasions we must draw on Christ's strength and God's ability to become our defense.

God told Moses in the 23rd chapter of Exodus that "I will be an enemy unto your enemies and an adversary to your adversaries." God also encourages us in the 23rd Psalm that even though we may walk through the valley of the shadow of death that we need not fear. He will be there to protect and guide us.

Now, granted, it is quite natural to want to defend ourselves in situations where our reputation has been trashed, or where we have been misrepresented or misunderstood. But it is not always possible to do that. There is no human way to stop gossip that has passed through the mouths of many people.

Gossip, slander, and various forms of harsh words can be likened to cutting open a feather pillow and shaking out the feathers on a very windy day. They blow in every which direction. Some of the feathers stick in the trees, on bushes, and in the mud. Trying to gather each feather and put them back into the pillow is absolutely impossible.

The reputation of Jesus was ridiculed and attacked. He was physically assaulted, tortured, and killed in our place. Yet, in all of this He opened not his mouth in revenge or retribution, or to defend Himself. He could have spoken a word, or called angels to His defense, but He chose to remain silent. He chose to not defend himself, His followers, or His ministry. He placed His present and future into the hands of Almighty God. It's very human to be self-defensive. It's very divine to let God be your defender and leave your present circumstances and future plans in His hands.

It has been said that, "a best defense is a good offense." Our best offense for the difficulties of life is to have Christ as our defender. Are you at a place where you are ready to trust Christ to rise to your defense?

> *Don't let them say, "Look! We have what we wanted! Now we will eat him alive!" May those who rejoice at my troubles be humiliated and disgraced. May those who triumph over me be covered with shame and dishonor. But give great joy to those who have stood with me in my defense. Let them continually say, "Great is the LORD, who enjoys helping his servant." Then I will tell everyone of your justice and goodness, and I will praise you all day long.*
>
> Psalm 35:25-28 NLT

Jesus, Lover of My Soul

Jesus, Lover of my soul,
  let me to Thy bosom fly,
While the nearer waters roll,
  while the tempest still is high;
Hide me, O my Savior,
  hide, till the storm of life is past;
Safe into the heaven guide;
  O receive my soul at last!

Other refuge have I none;
  hangs my helpless soul on Thee;
Leave, ah! Leave me not alone,
  still support and comfort me.
All my trust on Thee is stayed;
  all my help from Thee I bring;
Cover my defenseless head
  with the shadow of Thy wing.

Thou, O Christ, art all I want;
  more than all in Thee I find;
Raise the fallen, cheer the faint,
  heal the sick, and lead the blind.
Just and holy is Thy name;
  I am all unrighteousness;
False and full of sin I am;
  Thou art full of truth and grace.

cont'd.

Plenteous grace with Thee is found,
   grace to cover all my sin;
Let the healing streams abound;
   make and keep me pure within.
Thou of life the fountain are;
   freely let me take of Thee:
Spring Thou up within my heart;
   rise to all eternity.

Hymn by Charles Wesley, 1740

Christ-Likeness

Being Self-Conscious can be damaging, detrimental, and dangerous. The author C. S. Lewis made the observation that, "no man who says, 'I'm as good as you,' believes it. He would not say it if he did. The Saint Bernard never says it to the toy dog, nor the scholar to the dunce, nor the employable to the bum, nor the pretty woman to the plain. The claim to equality is made only by those who feel themselves to be in some way inferior. What it expresses is the itching, smarting awareness of an inferiority which the patient refuses to accept, and therefore resents." The Bible says, "Before his downfall a man's heart is proud, but humility comes before honor" (Proverbs 18:12).

Self-Denial on the other hand is positive, practical, and productive. Bruce Barton said, "It is when we forget ourselves that we do things that are most likely to be remembered. What a curious phenomenon it is that you can get men to die for the liberty of the world who will not make the little sacrifice that is needed to free themselves from their own individual bondage." As we mentioned earlier, the Bible recommends that we, "Do nothing out of selfish ambition or vain conceit, but in humility consider others better than yourselves. Each of you should look not only to your own interests, but also to the interests of others" (Philippians 2:3-4).

Life does not compensate us for insight, understanding, wisdom, or intention. It only rewards action. I can tell the Internal Revenue Service that I intended to pay my taxes, but all they care about is the money. I can tell my wife that I understand how tired she is, but she would rather I did the dishes. I can tell my mechanic that I have gained much insight as to how an internal combustion engine runs, but all he will ask is, "Did you put oil in it?" I can tell my children that I read a book and acquired much wisdom on being a father, but all they care about is if I attended their soccer game.

Henry Ford said, "You can't build a reputation on what you intended to do." We can easily get wrapped up in mind games and forget practical, daily living.

Much of life is spent in facing the issues of self-denial. To have a healthy family, I have to sometimes give up what I would like to personally do. I may desire to watch a sports program on TV, but I give it up to teach my daughter how to ride a bike. I might like to get some sleep, but my child may be crying and I have to get up to change a diaper. My spouse might need some time away from the children. This means I might have to give up a particular project I'm working on and focus on babysitting. So what else is new? These types of things happen all the time.

Often we have to face choices. Do I eat a second helping of food or watch my diet? Do I lie around on the couch and look at a new movie or go outside and get some exercise? Do I go back to school to better myself or do I just sit around thinking about how to get rich quick? Do I spend my extra money on a boat or save the same money for retirement? Many of these decisions boil down to the issue of do I want to have instant gratification of my desires or delayed gratification? Do I want to indulge in my own selfishness or seek to meet the needs of others? This is a never ending battle throughout life.

Paul addressed the battle between right and wrong, good and evil this way in Romans 7:15-25:

> *I don't understand myself at all, for I really want to do what is right, but I can't. I do what I don't want to—what I hate. I know perfectly well that what I am doing is wrong, and my bad conscience proves that I agree with these laws I am breaking. But I can't help myself because I'm no longer doing it. It is sin inside me that is stronger than I am that makes me do these evil*

> *things. I know I am rotten through and through so far as my old sinful nature is concerned. No matter which way I turn I can't make myself do right. I want to but I can't. When I want to do good, I don't; and when I try not to do wrong, I do it anyway. Now if I am doing what I don't want to, it is plain where the trouble is: sin still has me in its evil grasp.*
>
> *It seems to be a fact of life that when I want to do what is right, I inevitably do what is wrong. I love to do God's will so far as my new nature is concerned; but there is something else deep within me, in my lower nature, that is at war with my mind and wins the fight and makes me a slave to the sin that is still within me. In my mind I want to be God's willing servant, but instead I find myself still enslaved to sin. So you see how it is: my new life tells me to do right, but the old nature that is still inside me lives to sin. Oh, what a terrible predicament I'm in! Who will free me from the slavery to this deadly lower nature: Thank God! It has been done by Jesus Christ our Lord. He has set me free.*

To demonstrate Christ-Likeness—dynamic, matchless, and life-giving—Paul the Apostle suggests that:

> *Your attitude should be the same as that of Christ Jesus: who, being in very nature God, did not consider equality with God something to be grasped, but made himself nothing, taking the very nature of a servant, being made in human likeness. And being found in appearance as a man, he humbled himself and became obedient*

> *to death—even death on a cross!* (Philippians 2:5-8)
>
> *Then Jesus said to his disciples, "If anyone would come after me, he must deny himself and take up his cross and follow me. For whoever wants to save his life will lose it, but whoever loses his life for me will find it. What good will it be for a man if he gains the whole world, yet forfeits his soul?"* (Matthew 16:24-26)

I am reminded of the story of the young man who wanted to become very wise and used of God. He traveled all over the world talking with people seeking advice. One day he heard that there was an extremely wise and godly man who lived in the mountains of Mexico.

After many days of travel, the young man came upon the house of the wise man. He knocked and the old man opened the door. The young man introduced himself and asked the old man if he was the person he was looking for. The old man carefully looked at the young man and said, "Perhaps."

For several days the young man told his story of his search for wisdom and how to be a godly man. The old man listened quietly. Finally the young man ran out of words and said, "Do you have any wise thoughts for me?"

The old man said, "Perhaps." He then motioned for the young man to follow him. They walked down a path toward a beautiful lake.

Upon arriving the young man said, "This is breathtaking. Is this where I can obtain wisdom?"

"Perhaps," said the old man.

The old man took the young man to the side of the lake and said, "Bend over and look carefully into the dark water." The young man got on his knees, bent over, and peered into the water. He could see his own face in the reflection of the still water. Suddenly, the old man pushed the young man's head under water. He struggled to break free but could not because the old man was very strong. Soon he could feel himself starting to lose consciousness from the lack of air.

At that point, the old man pulled the young man's head out of the water. The young man gasped for air and yelled, "What are you doing? You almost killed me! You're crazy!"

"Perhaps," said the old man. "But when you truly search for wisdom and godliness as you were fighting for air, then you will become wise."

Jesus is our example of wisdom, godliness, and a life lived with self-denial because of his great love for us. What has your search for wisdom and godliness been like?

Jesus My Glory

Oh Lord God, You have commanded me to believe in Jesus;
And I would flee to no other refuge,
wash in no other fountain,
build on no other foundation,
receive from no other fullness,
rest in no other relief.

His water and blood were not severed in their flow at the cross, may they never
be separated in my creed and experiences;

May I be equally convinced of the guilt and pollution of sin,
feel my need of a prince and savior,
implore of him repentance as well as forgiveness,
love holiness, and be pure in heart,
have the mind of Jesus, and tread in his steps.

Let me not be at my own disposal, but rejoice that I am under the care of one who is
too wise to err,
too kind to injure,
too tender to crush,

May I scandalize none by my temper and conduct, but recommend and endear Christ to all around,
bestow good on every one as circumstances permit,
and decline no opportunity of usefulness.

Grant that I may value my substance,
not as the medium of pride and luxury,
but as the means of my support and stewardship.

cont'd.

It's All About Jesus

Help me to guide my affections with discretion,
to owe no man anything,
to be able to give to him that is in need,
to feel it my duty and pleasure to be merciful and forgiving,
to show to the world the likeness of Jesus.

Early Puritan Prayer

Turn Your Eyes Upon Jesus

O soul, are you weary and troubled?
No light in the darkness you see?
There's light for a look at the Savior,
And life more abundant and free!

Turn your eyes upon Jesus,
Look full in His wonderful face,
And the things of earth
Will grow strangely dim
In light of His glory and grace.

Through death into life everlasting
He passed, and we follow Him there;
Over us sin no more hath dominion
For more than conquerors we are!

His word shall not fail you—He promised;
Believe Him, and all will be well;
Then go to a world that is dying,
His perfect salvation to tell!

Hymn by Helen H. Lemmel, 1922

Christ-Empowered

Self-Despair creates emotions that are damaging, detrimental, and dangerous. Despair is an extreme state of hopelessness that eats away our happiness like a vulture. It sometimes occurs when our own expectations are not realized. Comtesse Diane speaks of this when she says. "We all think we are exceptional, and are surprised to find ourselves criticized just like anyone else." The Bible is written to encourage those who are discouraged. *"Why are you downcast, O my soul? Why so disturbed within me? Put your hope in God, for I will yet praise him, my Savior and my God"* (Psalm 42:1).

"For I know the plans I have for you," declares the LORD, "plans to prosper you and not to harm you, plans to give you hope and a future. Then you will call upon me and come and pray to me, and I will listen to you. You will seek me and find me when you seek me with all your heart. I will be found by you," declares the LORD" (Jeremiah 29:11-14).

Self-Discipline on the other hand is positive, practical, and productive. It helps to drive away self-despair. Harry Emerson Fosdick recommended that, "No steam or gas ever drives anything until it is confined. No Niagara is ever turned into light and power until it is tunneled. No life ever grows until it is focused, dedicated, disciplined." The Bible says, *"For God did not give us a spirit of timidity, but a spirit of power, of love and of self-discipline"* (2 Timothy 1:7).

I am reminded of a story that James MacDonald shares in his book, *I Really Want to Change . . . So, Help me, God*. It is the story of Raynald, who was a fourteenth century duke in Belgium. Raynald eventually became the king of Belgium, but his brother Edward was very jealous. Edward convinced a group to follow him and they overthrew Raynald's kingship. But Edward had compassion for Raynald and did not put him to death. Instead, he designed a special dungeon for him. It was a large circular room with one regular-sized doorway. It was outfitted with a bed, a table, and a chair. He included all the essentials that Raynald would need to be fairly comfortable.

When the dungeon was completely built *around* Raynald, Edward paid him a visit. Edward pointed to the regular-sized doorway and called Raynald's attention to the fact that there was no door in the opening. A door was not necessary to keep Raynald in the dungeon because he was grossly overweight and too fat to squeeze through the opening. Edward then said to Raynald, "When you can fit through the doorway, you can leave."

King Edward then instructed his servants to bring massive platters of meats and other delicacies and daily place them on the table in Raynald's round dungeon room. The servants also filled the table with various kinds of pies and pastries. Many people accused Edward of being cruel, but he would respond, "My brother is not a prisoner. He can leave when he chooses to."

Now for the rest of the story: "Raynald remained in that same room, a prisoner of his own appetite, for more than ten years. He wasn't released until after Edward died in battle. By then his own health was so far gone that he died within a year—not because he had no choice but because he would not use his power to choose what was best for his life."

Noah Webster defines self-discipline as a "planned control and training of oneself for the sake of development." Self-discipline is most often a painful experience because we may have to give up something. Or we may have to learn a new skill that takes much emotional, intellectual, or physical energy. It takes strength of determination.

If we are going to *develop*, as Webster suggests, it means that we must make some type of change in our lives. Actually, change is not an option. It is an automatic, ongoing, lifelong, daily experience. *How* we change is our only option. Change begins by choosing, and choosing creates more change. You and you alone are the author of the choice.

To make positive changes in your life you must begin by doing something differently—especially if what you are doing presently is not bringing happiness. You cannot ride a bike until you get on it. You can't learn to swim by standing on the shore. You can't catch a fish until you put the hook into the water. You can't eat carrots until you plant them. Talking about something does not bring results.

You must take action. This is the cause-and-effect principle. "If you do different, you will have different. If you do the same, you will have the same." This is the sowing and reaping truth that Paul talked about in Galatians 6:7-9.

> *Don't be misled; remember that you can't ignore God and get away with it: a man will always reap just the kind of crop he sows! If he sows to please his own wrong desires, he will be planting seeds of evil and he will surely reap a harvest of spiritual decay and death; but if he plants the good things of the Spirit, he will reap the everlasting life that the Holy Spirit gives him. And let us not get tired of doing what is right, for after a while we will reap a harvest of blessing if we don't get discouraged and give up.*

Men and women define themselves by action. She is a mother because she mothers. He is a carpenter because he builds houses. She is a soccer player because she plays. No one is a mother, carpenter, or soccer player without the accompanying actions. We are what we do. John Locke expressed it this way, "The actions of men are the best interpreters of their thoughts."

I am an angry person because I hold and display angry thoughts and actions. I am a depressed person because I display hopeless thoughts and actions. I am a critical person because I display critical thoughts and actions. We cannot separate the two. Jesus even said:

> *All of you listen . . . and try to understand. Your souls aren't harmed by what you eat, but by what you think and say! . . . It is the thought life that pollutes. For from within, out of men's hearts, come evil thoughts of lust, theft, murder, adultery, wanting what belongs to others, wickedness, deceit, lewdness, envy, slander, pride, and all other folly. All these vile things come from within; they are what pollute you and make you unfit for God.* (Mark 7:14-15, 20-23)

James the brother of Jesus said, "Therefore, to one who knows the right thing to do and does not do it, to him it is sin." You see, it is possible to have the knowledge of right and wrong, good and bad, and still not do it.

How are you doing in the area of self-discipline? Are there things you should be doing that you're not? Or, the reverse, are you doing something that needs to be stopped? Does your thinking pattern need an overhaul? Change, growth, and development do not come easily. Someone has said, "The only one who likes change is a baby with a wet diaper."

Focusing on becoming Christ-Empowered is dynamic, matchless, and life-giving. Paul the apostle said:

> *Do you not know that those who run in a race all run, but one receives the prize? Run in such a way that you may obtain it. And everyone who competes for the prize is temperate in all things. Now they do it to obtain a perishable crown, but we for an imperishable crown. Therefore I run thus: not with uncertainty. Thus I fight: not as one who beats the air. But I discipline my body*

> *and bring it into subjection, lest, when I have preached to others, I myself should become disqualified.* (1 Corinthians 9:24-27)

> *For God did not give us a spirit of timidity, but a spirit of power, of love and of self-discipline.* (2 Timothy 1:7)

Years ago I was a lifeguard. My job was to watch for swimmers who were in trouble and rescue them if necessary. Good swimmers and bad swimmers are easily distinguished from one another. A good swimmer places one hand after another in the water following the centerline of his or her body. The hand strokes seem to fall one on top of the other as they move forward.

A poor swimmer does not stroke following the centerline. Their hands hit the water right in front of each shoulder. When they get into trouble, their hand strokes begin to flail about, even going out to their sides. They are grasping for straws or anything that will keep them afloat.

A good lifeguard will not attempt to rescue poor swimmers until they come to the end of their strength and give up. Rescuers know that if they get too close, the swimmer will have enough strength to drown both of them in the midst of the rescue operation.

The same concept is true for many situations in life. Jesus would like to rescue you from emotional hurts, intellectual doubts, and destroying habits. However, He knows that you must first come to the end of your own strength. He patiently waits till you get tired enough with your own efforts and give up.

Change and growth often come when you get to the point where you allow Jesus to take over your situation. Jesus said, "Come to me, all of you who are weary and carry heavy burdens, and I will give you rest. Take my yoke upon you. Let me teach you, because I am humble and gentle, and you will find rest for your souls. For my yoke fits perfectly, and the burden I give you is light."

Are you weary and tired? Have you been carrying a heavy burden? Are you ready to give up on your own strength? Would you like to change? Jesus has been patiently waiting for you to run to his open arms.

In Psalm 18 David speaks of God's rescue operation for a tired soul:

> *I love you, O LORD, my strength. The LORD is my rock, my fortress and my deliverer; My God is my rock, in whom I take refuge. He is my shield and the horn of my salvation, my stronghold. I call to the LORD, who is worthy of praise, and I am saved from my enemies. The cords of death entangled me; the torrents of destruction overwhelmed me. The cords of the grave coiled around me; the snares of death confronted me.*
>
> *In my distress I called to the LORD; I cried to my God for help. From his temple he heard my voice; my cry came before him, into his ears. The earth trembled and quaked, and the foundations of the mountains shook; they trembled because he was angry. Smoke rose from his nostrils; consuming fire came from his mouth, burning coals blazed out of it.*
>
> *He parted the heavens and came down; dark clouds were under his feet. He mounted the cherubim and flew; he soared on the wings of the wind. He made darkness his covering, his canopy around him—the dark rain clouds of the*

sky. Out of the brightness of his presence clouds advanced, with hailstones and bolts of lightning.

The LORD thundered from heaven; the voice of the Most High resounded. He shot his arrows and scattered [the enemies], great bolts of lightning and routed them. The valleys of the sea were exposed and the foundations of the earth laid bare at your rebuke, O LORD, at the blast of breath from your nostrils.

He reached down from on high and took hold of me; he drew me out of deep waters. He rescued me from my powerful enemy, from my foes, who were too strong for me. They confronted me in the day of my disaster, but the LORD was my support. He brought me out into a spacious place; he rescued me because he delighted in me . . .

As for God, his way is perfect; the word of the LORD is flawless.

He is a shield for all who take refuge in him. For who is God besides the LORD? And who is the Rock except our God? It is God who arms me with strength and makes my way perfect. He makes my feet like the feet of a deer; he enables me to stand on the heights. He trains my hands for battle; my arms can bend a bow of bronze. You give me your shield of victory, and your right hand sustains me; you stoop down to make me great. You broaden the path beneath me, so that my ankles do not turn.

The Love of God

The love of God is greater far,
Than tongue or pen can ever tell,
It goes beyond the highest star
And reaches to the lowest hell;
The guilty pair bowed down with care,
God gave His Son to win;
His erring child He reconciled
And pardoned from his sin.

When years of time shall pass away
And earthly thrones and kingdoms fall,
When men, who here refuse to pray
On rocks and hills and mountains call;
God's love so sure shall still endure,
All measureless and strong;
Redeeming grace to Adam's race
The saints' and angels' song.

Could we with ink the ocean fill
And were the skies of parchment made,
Were every stalk on earth a quill
And every man a scribe by trade.
To write the love of God above
Would drain the ocean dry;
Nor could the scroll contain the whole
Though stretched the sky to sky.

Hymn by Frederick M. Lehman, 1917

Christ-Forgiven

Attempting to become Self-Important can be very damaging, detrimental, and dangerous. Desderius Erasmus tells the story of Plato entertaining some friends in a room where there was a couch richly ornamented. Diogenes came in very dirty, as usual, and getting upon the couch, and trampling on it, said, "I trample upon the pride of Plato."

Plato mildly answered, "But with greater pride, Diogenes!"

Ann Landers brings it into the modern world when she says, "Know yourself. Don't accept your dog's admiration as conclusive evidence that you are wonderful." The Bible tells us that, *"Pride goes before destruction and haughtiness before a fall"* (Proverbs 16:18).

Exercising Self-Forgiveness can be positive, practical, and productive. William Wordsworth commented, "From the body of one guilty deed a thousand ghostly fears and haunting thoughts proceed." The writer of Psalm 38:4 puts it this way, "My guilt has overwhelmed me like a burden too heavy to bear."

Do you remember the first time you stole something? I do. My mother used to keep her coin purse near the telephone in the kitchen. One day it was open and I saw a lot of loose change. I wanted some money so I could buy some candy at the store. I was around five years of age.

I looked around to see if anyone was watching. Why do you think I did that? It was because of a God-given gift to every man and woman. It is called conscience. Conscience has the unique ability to tie together feelings with the knowledge of right and wrong. Conscience ascertains our duty before we proceed to action. It is a built-in judgment court that either accuses us or excuses us of the thoughts and behaviors we are about to do—or of behaviors and thoughts we have already done.

Cowardice asks, Is it safe? Expediency asks, Is it politic?

Vanity asks, Is it popular? But Conscience asks, Is it right?

William Morley Punshon

Conscience, true as the needle to the pole, points steadily to the pole-star of God's eternal justice, reminding the soul of the fearful realities of the life to come.

Ezra Hall Gillett

Conscience is the root of all true courage; if a man would be brave let him obey his conscience.

James Freeman Clarke

Well, the fact of the matter is that I didn't listen to my conscience. I took five pennies and went to the store. Then I began to feel a new emotion. It was called guilt. The ancient writer Seneca describes guilt this way: "Let wickedness escape as it may at the bar (of justice), it never fails of doing justice upon itself; for every guilty person is his own hangman."

Thinking I was pretty clever, I put ten pieces of candy into my pocket and went to the cashier. I pulled out five pieces of candy and put down five pennies. My heart was beating out of my chest. Would it work? Would I be caught?

The cashier took the money and I left the store. I started to walk down the alley behind the store thinking, *It worked*. I reached into my pocket and pulled out a piece of my stolen treasure. I was about to put it into my mouth when I heard a voice behind me. It was another store keeper who had witnessed my theft. Now my heart really began to beat. I was caught in the act. I was guilty of a double theft and I knew it.

Are there any events in your past that you're regretting? Things you've done or said? Or things you should have done or said that you didn't? Regret can take the form of guilt, sorrow, loss, or remorse. Rolling around in the mud puddle of regret solves nothing. You only get dirtier and slip and fall more often. Rebecca Beard suggests, "We should have no regrets. The past is finished. There is nothing to be gained by going over it. Whatever it gave us in the experiences it brought us was something we had to know."

The question is, *What have you learned?* Have you learned, "Do not be deceived; God is not mocked, for whatever a man sows, that he will also reap. For he who sows to his own flesh will from the flesh reap corruption; but he who sows to the Spirit will from the Spirit reap eternal life" (Galatians 6:7-8).

Have you learned that you need to forgive yourself? Have you realized that you are not perfect and that you have faults just like everyone else? When we come to the realization that we have missed the mark we can do one of two things:

We can experience misery, anger, fear, depression, and frustration and attempt to live up to some standard that we can never obtain . . .

Or we can acknowledge that we can never reach the high standard of perfection. We need help to right the wrongs that we have committed against ourselves, others, and God.

> *What shall we say, then? Shall we go on sinning so that grace may increase? By no means! We died to sin; how can we live in it any longer? Or don't you know that all of us who were baptized into Christ Jesus were baptized into his death? We were therefore buried with him through baptism into death in order that, just as Christ was raised from the dead through the glory of the Father, we too may live a new life.*

If we have been united with him like this in his death, we will certainly also be united with him in his resurrection. For we know that our old self was crucified with him so that the body of sin might be done away with, that we should no longer be slaves to sin—because anyone who has died has been freed from sin.

Now if we died with Christ, we believe that we will also live with him. For we know that since Christ was raised from the dead, he cannot die again; death no longer has mastery over him. The death he died, he died to sin once for all; but the life he lives, he lives to God.

In the same way, count yourselves dead to sin but alive to God in Christ Jesus. Therefore do not let sin reign in your mortal body so that you obey its evil desires. Do not offer the parts of your body to sin, as instruments of wickedness, but rather offer yourselves to God, as those who have been brought from death to life; and offer the parts of your body to him as instruments of righteousness. For sin shall not be your master, because you are not under law, but under grace. (Romans 6:1-14)

To be Christ-Forgiven is dynamic, matchless, and life giving. Thomas Fuller observed that, "He that cannot forgive others breaks the bridge over which he must pass himself; for every man has need to be forgiven." The Bible instructs us that, "If you forgive those who sin against you, your heavenly Father will forgive you. But if you refuse to forgive others, your Father will not forgive your sins" (Matthew 6:14-15).

Have you ever wondered why forgiveness is so difficult? It's because the injured party lets the person who has done the injury go free. Archibald Hart says it this way: "Forgiveness is surrendering my right to hurt you back if you hurt me." Mark Twain expressed the same concept when he stated: "Forgiveness is the fragrance the violet sheds on the heel that has crushed it."

Let's say I came over to your house to visit. You invite me in, and we go into your living room. You say, "Please sit down." For some reason I choose not to sit in a big soft chair but instead sit down in a small rocking chair. Before you can speak, the small rocking chair collapses under my weight. You see, I didn't know it was an antique rocking chair that had been handed down through your family. To you it was a "display" piece in your home. Everyone is shocked and I feel like an idiot.

I say, "I'm sorry. Can I buy you another one?"

"No." you reply.

"Can I replace it for you?"

"No," you say with sadness and pain in your voice.

"Will you forgive me?"

Inside, you groan with pain.

Can you see why forgiveness is so difficult? The person who inflicts the injury goes free, leaving the injured party in pain and misery. This is a dirty deal, and it is not fair. It's not a pleasant experience in the least. Repayment for the offense is impossible. I cannot put the broken chair back into the same condition it was before the accident. Any revenge you might want to express will not replace the chair. Resenting me for breaking the chair will not restore it. In forgiveness, the injured party has to make peace with the pain and accept the loss. This is why most people do not like to forgive—it's too costly and too painful.

Forgiveness is not the denial of the emotions of hurt and anger. Forgiveness does not repress and hold down feelings. Forgiveness does not suppress the fullness of the pain.

Forgiveness does not ask us to pretend that everything is fine and to act nice when a problem does exist.

Forgiveness is very realistic. Forgiveness is honest; it does not hide its head in the sand, thinking that difficulties will go away if they're not acknowledged. Forgiveness does not fantasize that what is unchangeable can be changed or undone.

Forgiveness does not passively accept or condone unacceptable behavior. It does not rationalize, give alibis, or make excuses for the offending party. It is not a doormat for evil to continue unconfronted. Forgiveness is not afraid to exercise tough love and the truth. Forgiveness is not afraid to talk about repentance, restoration, and reconciliation. It is not an emotional umbilical cord that allows the offending party to avoid personal responsibility.

Forgiveness is not isolation from the person who has done the offending. It does not take the attitude of superiority or piously hand out pity to the offender. Forgiveness does not place blame or make the other person feel guilty.

> *You must make allowance for each other's faults and forgive the person who offends you. Remember, the Lord forgave you, so you must forgive others.* (Colossians 3:12-13)

Forgiveness does not come by accident. It is a choice. It is an attitude. It is a process. It is a way of life. Forgiveness is not an emotion. If people had to wait until they felt like forgiving others, pigs would fly first. Forgiveness is found in the will. It is a promise; it is a commitment to three things, as Jay E. Adams suggests:

I will not use the event against them in the future.
I will not talk to others about them.
I will not dwell on it myself.

Forgiveness does not beat the offending party over the head

with their offense, trying to make them feel guilty. It does not try to destroy the reputation of the offending party or get revenge by sharing the transgression with others. Forgiveness does not wallow in the misery of the conflict. It gets up and moves on with life. It does not rip off the scabs to see if the offense is healing, for this only prolongs the hurt.

Does all of this sound difficult? It is. It's exactly what Jesus did for us when we [the guilty parties] were set free from the penalty of our sins . . . and He died in our place. If He can do that for us cannot we, in turn, forgive those who offend us?

Clara Barton, the founder of the American Red Cross, was once reminded of an especially cruel thing that had been done to her years before. "I don't recall that incident," she replied. "Don't you remember it?" her friend asked. "No," came the reply. "I distinctly remember forgetting the incident."

> *Blessed are they whose transgressions are forgiven, whose sins are covered. Blessed is the man whose sin the Lord will never count against him.* (Romans 4:7-8)

Christ-Awareness

Being self-interested can be damaging, detrimental, and dangerous. I'm reminded of the old fable of King Midas. He's a classic example of a person absorbed in his own self-interest. As you recall, he was granted one wish. After a few moments of thought he said, "For my wish, I would like everything I touch to turn to solid gold."

You see, Midas was very greedy. He enjoyed the things money could buy. He also reveled in the power that so often goes along with those who are rich. And as an added bonus, he loved all the attention he got for being so wealthy.

However, there is one thing King Midas didn't take into consideration. It was the fact that *everything* turned to gold. When he touched a servant, he turned to gold. When he touched an animal, it turned to gold. When he touched loved ones, they turned to gold. When he became hungry and reached for some food, it turned to gold also.

It has been said, there is no fire like passion, there is no shark like hatred, there is no snare like folly, and there is no torrent like greed. Self-interest, like the gold of King Midas, has a way of destroying everyone around us.

Now, for the rest of the story. King Midas begged to have his wish for gold taken away. However, you will remember, that as a punishment for his greed he was given donkey's ears for the rest of his life. He then had a special crown made to hide his donkey's ears. Only his barber knew the strange and funny secret.

The barber desperately wanted to share what he knew about the king but he knew that he would lose his life if he did. Instead, he dug a hole in the ground and whispered into it, "King Midas has donkey's ears." Then he quickly covered the hole and went home feeling somewhat relieved. The next spring the flowers bloomed and began to sing together, "King Midas has donkey's ears . . . King Midas has donkey's ears."

The parallel is there for our lives. Our greedy self-interest destroys those around us. At some point, our selfishness will get exposed to others. They will talk and gossip about us. In the end, our self interest does not even satisfy us. There is a proverb that says, "He who lives only to benefit himself confers on the whole world a benefit when he dies."

Self-knowledge on the other hand can be positive, practical, and productive.

St. Augustine commented, "People travel to wonder at the height of mountains, at the huge waves of the sea, at the long courses of rivers, at the vast compass of the ocean, at the circular motion of the stars, and they pass by themselves without wonder."

It is good to know those things that irritate you. It is beneficial to be aware of your skills, talents, and special abilities. It is also helpful to have plans for the future as to the career you would like to follow.

It is wise to be aware of your weak spots too. One of our American founding fathers, William Penn, addressed the concept of human weaknesses when he said, "If thou wouldst conquer thy weakness thou must never gratify it. No man is compelled to evil; only his consent makes it his. It is no sin to be tempted; it is to yield and be overcome."

How does one come to the point of beginning to deal with weaknesses? It comes about in direct proportion to how aware of Jesus we are.

To exercise Christ-awareness is dynamic, life changing, and matchless.

The starting point for Christ-awareness begins with a personal encounter with Jesus. How does that take place? Jesus, himself, said, "Behold, I stand at the door and knock. If anyone hears My voice and opens the door, I will come in to him and dine with him, and he with Me."

Paul the Apostle amplified on this thought when he said, "The word is near you, in your mouth and in your heart (that is, the word of faith which we preach): that if you confess with your mouth the Lord Jesus and believe in your heart that God has raised Him from the dead, you will be saved. For with the heart one believes unto righteousness, and with the mouth confession is made to salvation . . . For whoever calls on the name of the Lord shall be saved."

So Did I

I was caught within the center of a milling, frenzied mob
That spat upon and ridiculed the unflinching Son of God.
I beheld them as they mocked Him, and I heard their taunting cry
As they jeered Him in their madness . . . and as they did . . . So did I.

On His head with brutal fingers, they did thrust a thorny crown,
And the maddened mob roared louder as the blood came trickling down.
With the lashes then they scourged Him while the mob cried "Crucify!"
Dragging forth the heavy crosses . . . and as they did . . . So did I.

Through the crowded streets they led Him to a hill without the wall,
And the crowd that lately cheered Him loudly scoffed now at His fall.
Then I heard the sound of hammers and I watched the crosses rise
To a cry of hate full throated . . . and as they did . . . So did I.

Nearer to the cross, and nearer; did I work my way apace
Till I reached the feet of Jesus and could look upon His face.
Then my lips forgot their mocking, and I felt my hatred die.
When the thief beside sought pardon . . . as the thief did . . . So did I.

Then He healed my every heartache; with His blood purged out my sin;
Promised me a life eternal; gave me perfect peace within.
On the path where earnest Christians struggle daily to draw nigh
To the perfect rest of Heaven . . . Well, as they do . . . So shall I.

cont'd.

It's All About Jesus

With my cross I'll follow Jesus, let the mob do as it will;
Though it heap abuse upon me in His steps I'll follow still.
Step by step I'll follow Jesus, though the clouds bedim the sky
And the martyr's death awaits me . . . yet, as they died . . . So can I.

When at last the zero hour marks the ending of the age
And the angel who recorded blots the fatal, final page . . .
Then the trumpet loud will signal, in the twinkling of an eye
As the saved of earth go upward . . . as the saved go . . . So shall I.

Author Unknown

The second way we become aware of Christ is to read the Bible. The Bible points to Christ and it describes who He is and what he wants to do for us. The Bible is our guidebook for daily living, our map to Heaven, and our comfort is the tough times of life. The humorist Mark Twain even said, "It ain't those parts of the Bible that I can't understand that bother me, it is the parts that I do understand."

The third avenue for becoming aware of Christ is through the Holy Spirit. Jesus in the Book of John, chapters 15 and 16, refers to the Holy Spirit as our comforter.

> But when the Helper comes, whom I shall send to you from the Father, the Spirit of truth who proceeds from the Father, He will testify of Me. I still have many things to say to you, but you cannot bear them now. However, when He, the Spirit of truth, has come, He will guide you into all truth; for He will not speak on His own authority, but whatever He hears He will speak; and He will tell you things to come. He will glorify Me, for He will take of what is Mine and declare it to you. All things that the Father has are Mine. Therefore I said that He will take of Mine and declare it to you.

It's All About Jesus

The Holy Spirit uses four primary ways to speak to our hearts and give us direction for daily living.

1. He speaks through the pages of the Bible.

2. He brings people into our lives to give us advice and direction.

3. He uses circumstances to help course-correct us.

4. He uses the still small voice of conscience to speak to us.

How attentive and aware of Jesus are you? Do you follow the quiet voice of conscience? Jesus makes us aware of His presence by placing thoughts into our minds.

- You spoke roughly to your spouse . . . you need to apologize.

- You should not be looking at pornography on the Internet . . . you need to turn it off.

- You should speak a kind word to that person . . . they need a friendly touch from someone who cares.

- You need to think about your family's needs . . . you are being selfish.

- You need to be studying the Bible . . . it will help you grow.

A number of years ago, quite a few people used to wear

what is called a WWJD bracelet. It stood for, **W**hat **W**ould **J**esus **D**o? The more we ask ourselves that same question the more aware of Jesus we become.

- When we get into a conflict situation ask, **W**hat **W**ould **J**esus **D**o?
- When a person needs some emotional help ask, **W**hat **W**ould **J**esus **D**o?
- When a community service opportunity presents itself ask, **W**hat **W**ould **J**esus **D**o?
- When we are presented with a financial need for a charity ask, **W**hat **W**ould **J**esus **D**o?
- When someone requests prayer support ask, **W**hat **W**ould **J**esus **D**o?
- When we meet a stranger who wants to talk and we are tired ask, **W**hat **W**ould **J**esus **D**o?

SUGGESTION: Write the phrase **W**hat **W**ould **J**esus **D**o? on a 3X5 card or a piece of paper. Pin it on your refrigerator. Put it on the dashboard of your car. Tape it on your computer. Carry it in your purse or wallet. Keep it somewhere as a reminder to become aware of Jesus on a daily basis in the midst of your busy life.

Christ Tapped Me On The Shoulder

Christ tapped me on the shoulder once when I was young . . . and free,
And all He said was, "Son, I wish you'd follow after me."
I know I should . . . but I had plans to strike out on my own
And felt that I could travel best if I went on . . . alone.

Christ tapped me on the shoulder, too, in nineteen fifty-eight
And all He said was, "Better come; the hour is getting late."
But I was rich and in my glance I knew that He could see
A look that said, "I have no need to follow after . . . Thee!"

Christ tapped me on the shoulder next when all my gold was gone;
There was but kindness in His voice He simply said . . . "Come on."
Had He been human, well He might have passed me quickly by;
Instead He smiled and I could sense compassion in His eye.

Christ taps me on the shoulder now a dozen times a day
For I have learned the joy that comes to those who walk His way.
To all these things I testify that all who hear may know
How glad I am, once when He called, I had the sense . . . to go!

Author Unknown

Beneath the Cross of Jesus

Beneath the cross of Jesus
I fain would take my stand—
The shadow of a mighty Rock
Within a weary land;
A home within the wilderness,
A rest upon the way,
From the burning of the noontide heat,
And the burden of the day.

Upon that cross of Jesus
Mine eye at times can see
The very dying form of One
Who suffered there for me;
And from my smitten heart with tears
Two wonders I confess—
The wonders of redeeming love
And my unworthiness.

I take, O cross, they shadow
For my abiding place;
I ask no other sunshine than
The sunshine of His face;
Content to let the world go by,
To know no gain nor loss,
My sinful self my only shame,
My glory all the cross.

Hymn by Elizabeth Cecelia Clephane, 1868

Part II
Our Stories of Grace:
Three Different Journeys to Jesus

Charlie "Tremendous" Jones

Therefore, if anyone is in Christ, he is a new creation; the old has gone, the new has come!
II Corinthians 5:17

Everyone is on an individual journey through life and no two people walk the same path. My particular story illustrates that your future has nothing to do with your past. I am also reminded that my past is always going to be the way it was. I cannot go back and rewrite it. I cannot change it. And I should stop trying to imagine it different than it was.

My early memories circle around times of laughter and games with my siblings. I can remember that during this time of life my parents seemed to care deeply for their children.

Like so many children born into poverty, I was blissfully unaware of our status until I was old enough to realize that our family was different from others. No one has the privilege to choose their country, their parents, or the circumstances they grow up in. As for our family, we lived in a back alley structure with no electricity or indoor plumbing.

My happiness, however, quickly faded when my mother disappeared. She had fallen in love with another man and left us all with one of the tenants at the little boarding house where she made meals for the local workers.

My mother returned four times over the next six years only to leave again and again. I was the oldest of five brothers and sisters. I could not understand why my mother left us. Didn't she love us?

Finally, in order to keep the children together, my father took a job with the Navy Seabees in the West Indies. His goal was to earn enough money to pay for the housekeepers to take care of all our basic needs. Unfortunately, our housekeepers had absolutely no use for children and, to make matters worse, some of them were relatives. Our relatives even treated us worse than the housekeepers.

I started earning my own spending money at six years of age by selling Liberty Magazines door to door. After that, I sold newspapers on the corner. When I was eight I discovered that other kids at school had parents who lived together. They were loved, well dressed, and played various sports. By the sixth grade, I was beginning to see the differences between their lives and mine. As a result I developed a tremendous inferiority complex. I desperately wanted to be accepted by my classmates. They had more opportunities than my siblings and I. They went to the weekly dances and had nice clothes to wear.

At twelve years of age, I got a part time job working in the local men's clothing store. I began to spend my earnings on nice clothes and was able to gradually be accepted by my peers. I also began to go to the teenage dances.

Despite all of my insecurity, I had a wonderful spirit of enthusiasm and desire to be better. I also had a strong ability to make friends.

At age thirteen, I got a job baking pies at four o'clock in the morning. I worked for three hours and then had one hour to walk the two miles to get to school. Naturally, I slept through most of my classes. While I had a talent and love for music and typing, I missed the basics with algebra and English and was totally lost in those subjects. I did so poorly in the 8th grade that I failed. I was totally humiliated as all my classmates and friends went on to high school and I did not. I had no parents to provide me with encouragement or guidance. I didn't return to school.

At 15, I decided I would lie about my age and go to another city for a laborer's job. I had heard that they were hiring and I arrived early in the morning with my sport coat and tie and wound up with all the older ditch diggers.

A lady came by and asked what I was doing in the line. I said I was waiting to apply for a ditch digger job. She asked me if I could type. I said yes and she asked me to come with her. I was hesitant and told her no, I didn't want to lose my spot in line. She said she'd take care of that and took me to her office at the Veteran's Hospital. They had just lost a secretary and needed someone to type the weekly patients' diagnoses. She said I'd be working for seven psychiatrists. I made another excuse and told her I couldn't do that. She finally said, "Will you try?"

It was then that I discovered my life's mantra and I said, *"I will."* I would, at the very least, always try. This was also important because it was the first experience I had of someone believing in me. This year of typing personal histories gave me insights into people and lives I never could have imagined. I also visited the patients who were confined to their wards for life, yet another powerful learning experience for me.

My father returned to the States and took a job with the Army Corps of Engineers. He knew that I was drinking and out of control and arranged to have me work with him at an Air Force Base in Alaska. From there on, my life went even deeper into sin. Finally, I turned eighteen and my father allowed me to come home to Pennsylvania and go out on my own.

I bought a pickup truck and decided to keep my evenings free for dancing and partying. During the day I used the truck to haul equipment and at night I used it to haul my friends to dance parties. We all learned that the local college was having its annual prom and we *loved* to crash proms. We all got part time jobs to earn money for tuxedos to impress our dates.

Our next step was to go to the YWCA sponsored dance to find our dates. It cost a dime which most of us paid. The ballroom was filled with beautiful girls.

At the start of the first dance I did not want to take any chances, so I went right to the one I wanted for the prom. Her name was Gloria. It was love at first sight. But we had a problem. She went to church regularly with her parents and I never went to church. I decided if I could only date her on Wednesday and Sunday, I would start going to church. Thirteen weeks later

I proposed to her. I told her I had nothing but if she would marry me I would spend my life trying to make her happy. To my surprise she said, "Yes."

We had no money and were not sure of her parent's approval, so we eloped in 1948. The next two years of my life were the happiest because I had someone who believed in me and I was totally committed and in love with her; however, this did nothing for the true emptiness I still felt in my soul.

In 1950, I ran into an old school mate, Jim, who had become a laundry truck driver. He saw me on the street and said, "Charlie, could we talk for a few minutes?" Well, I was a new life insurance salesman and was glad to talk to anyone. I thought that I might be able to sell Jim a policy. But Jim had a different idea. He spent the next thirty to forty minutes making me read scriptures to him out of a little Gideon New Testament.

I had been baptized in the church and worked hard at reforming myself, but I had no idea what it meant to be born again through God's word and receive the Holy Spirit.

After our talk, I found myself alone in my car. It was in Lancaster, Pennsylvania across from an old firehouse. I put my head down on the steering wheel and prayed. I admitted to God that I was a sinner and my life was in disarray. I wanted to surrender and yield my heart and receive Jesus as my savior as a gift from God. I immediately went home and told my wife what had happened. She could not believe it.

That week my younger sisters, for whom I was the guardian, took me to their little church. While there they asked me to teach a Sunday school class. I said I couldn't. They asked if I was a Christian and I said, "Yes." They asked if I knew two Bible verses. I said, "Yes." They said there were eight year old boys that needed a leader to love them, share two Bible verses with them, and teach them how to be born again. They then told me they would give me two wonderful books to help me teach the class. Even though I was scared to death I said, *"I will."*

And then I discovered in Christ, that the secret of success is found in the two simple words, *"I will."*

The next month the Sunday School Superintendent took me to the Christian Businessman's Dinner. I could not believe my eyes and ears. These men recited scripture, sang hymns with all their hearts, and soon became my new role models. I have enjoyed the Gideon's, Youth for Christ, and every organization that cared about men's souls.

I began to realize that past family upbringing and circumstances are not the important issues in life. It's about personally knowing Christ. It's about discovering all about Jesus as you gradually fade out of the picture. *"But thanks be to God, who always leads us in triumphal procession in Christ and through us spreads everywhere the fragrance of the knowledge of him"* (2 Corinthians 2:14).

I was born a nobody. I did not have the normal hugs, love, or encouragement like most children. But when you meet Christ, all of that is truly in the past.

I also realized that the bitterness and resentment I felt for my mother needed to be forgiven. I did not care about forgiving her at all before I met Christ. It was only after I realized how much Jesus had forgiven me that I, in turn, should forgive her. A tremendous burden of anger was lifted from my heart that day. I felt an unusual sense of peace as I let go of all the hurt I had been feeling.

I now thank the Lord. As I look back, I had no education. I had no steady parental role models. I had nothing except a future awaiting me . . . a tremendous future when I discovered that it's all about Jesus.

If I am going to know who Jesus is, I must obey Him. The majority of us don't know Jesus because we have not the remotest intention of obeying Him.

Oswald Chambers

Jesus, Thy Blood and Righteousness

Jesus, Thy blood and righteousness
My beauty are, my glorious dress;
Midst flaming worlds, in these arrayed,
With joy shall I lift up my head.

Bold shall I stand in Thy great day,
For who aught to my charge shall lay?
Fully absolved through these I am,
From sin and fear, from guilt and shame.

Lord, I believe Thy precious blood,
Which, at the mercy seat of God,
Forever doth for sinners plead,
For me, e'en for my soul, was shed.

Lord, I believe were sinners more
Than sands upon the ocean shore,
Thou hast for all a ransom paid,
For all a full atonement made.

Hymn by Nikolaus von Zinzendorf
Translated by John Wesley, 1740

Bob Phillips

Whoever drinks of the water I give him will never thirst. Indeed, the water I give him will become in him a spring of water welling up to everlasting life.

John 4:14

For the first fourteen years of my life I had an ongoing battle against the ravages of asthma. The struggle to get air during certain periods was my central focus. I can remember many nights sitting in a rocking chair as my mother held me near a steam kettle.

My parents and my brother and I lived in a basement that had been converted into an apartment. It was located under my mother's parents' home in Denver, Colorado. The windows we had were very narrow and high on the walls. They were located in window wells. The only thing we could see was the sky and the tops of a few trees.

The Second World War was in progress as I was very young. I have memories of my mother sitting in bed and crying time after time. I didn't know that she was crying because my father was overseas in Europe in the Air Force fighting the war with the possibility that he could be killed.

During the ten years we lived in the basement, I never conceived that we were moderately poor. It was not until I was much older that I realized that my parents could not afford to live elsewhere.

The basement included the heater room. The heater burned coal that was stored in a large cement bin outside of the house. A metal chute allowed the coal to drop into the heater room. Along with the coal came some unwelcome visitors: centipedes!

Centipedes have a pair of long antennae on their heads that

wiggle back and forth as they feel their way around. They also have two pairs of jaws. A full grown centipede has up to 170 pairs of legs and can be between two to three inches long. The first pair of legs, behind the head, has claws that are used for fighting rather than walking. These claws are called 'poison claws' and are filled with poison from a gland in the insect's head. Centipedes scurry very rapidly across the floor and up the walls and on the ceiling. They are not the most attractive creature in God's creation. They actually sort of give you the 'willies.'

As it happened, the bedroom that my brother and I slept in was next to the heater room. In fact, we had to pass through the heater room to get to our bedroom. It was in the passing through the heater room that I began to develop a fear of centipedes. There were many of them in the room.

I don't think I was afraid of them at first. I think the fear emerged when my older brother informed me that centipedes love to run up your body and into your ears to eat the wax out of them! That did it for me. I always ran through the heater room into our bedroom. I certainly didn't want that creature eating out of my head.

Along with the asthma, I wrestled with school. It was difficult for me especially when they pushed me forward a half a grade rather than holding me back. Seventh grade was not easy and the eighth became harder. It was in the ninth grade that I failed my first classes and had to go to summer school. Failure began to become a very familiar companion. In high school, it became worse. By the time it was over, I ended up failing thirteen courses. That caused me to go four years to a three-year high school. I can recall the teachers saying that I would never amount to much. On the positive side, I began to grow out of my difficulties with asthma.

During my early school years my mother took me to a church where they talked about Jesus Christ. I cannot remember a time when His name was not familiar to me. I heard that he was God's Son and that he died for everyone's sins. I accepted that concept without question but lived my life without consideration for what that meant. My knowledge of Jesus was strictly head knowledge. It was similar to knowing facts about any historical figure like George Washington or Theodore Roosevelt.

At eighteen I left home and moved to California. I went to a small junior college in the San Joaquin Valley. I was barely accepted because of my low grades in high school. It was while I was attending college that I had a small run-in with the law. The end result was that I was placed on a year's probation.

When I was about twenty years of age I was working at a camp at Hume Lake where I saw a girl that I thought I would like to get to know. She invited me to a meeting in the chapel. I went, not to get spiritual, but to strike up a relationship of some kind with her.

During the meeting the speaker challenged us with the thought that "either God was running our lives, or we were." I knew the answer to that question. I was running my life and it was a mess.

That night, I got alone with God down by a stream. As I sat on a log by myself I prayed, "God, I'm not sure if I know what it all means, but I would like you to come into my life and run it. I need you to change my life. I want you to take control." That night I was transformed by the grace of God.

I didn't hear any voices from heaven but I felt that something was different. I began to experience a sense of peace rather than turmoil. The change had begun.

The next day at work people began to say, "What happened to you?" The reason they asked that question was that I had a reputation for pranks and getting into trouble. I didn't always have an attitude of submission to authority. They must have sensed some kind of change.

I didn't know how to respond. All I could say was, "Last night I gave my life to Jesus."

Within a half a year after that, I applied to Biola University where I eventually graduated with a major in Christian Education and Bible and a minor in Psychology. It was at the university where I met my wife Pam. Several years later two daughters followed. As time passed, I went on for a Masters in Counseling and became a Marriage and Family Therapist. A couple of years later, I pursued a Ph.D. in Counseling. It was a far cry from my failures in high school!

What caused all of these changes? What stimulated and motivated me in a career path? What created peace out of turmoil? What helped to produce a submission to authority? It was a personal *heart* knowledge of Jesus rather than just a *head* knowledge. It was the realization that God loves me enough to send His Son to take away my disobedience and sin. It was the fact that Jesus gave me living water for a very thirsty soul. The bottom line is that it was all about Jesus living in me.

Tell Me the Story of Jesus

Tell me the story of Jesus,
Write on my heart every word;
Tell me the story most precious,
Sweetest that ever was heard.
Tell how the angels in chorus
Sang as they welcomed His birth,
"Glory to God in the highest!
Peace and good tidings to earth."

Tell me the story Jesus,
Write on my heart every word;
Tell me the story most precious,
Sweetest that ever was heard.

Fasting alone in the desert,
Tell of the days that are past,
How for our sins He was tempted,
Yet was triumphant at last.
Tell of the years of His labor,
Tell of the sorrow He bore,
He was despised and afflicted,
Homeless, rejected and poor.

Tell of the cross where they nailed Him,
Writhing in anguish and pain;
Tell of the grave where they laid Him,
Tell how He liveth again.
Love in that story so tender
Clearer than ever I see:
Lord, may I always remember
Love paid the ransom for me.

Hymn by Fanny Jane Crosby, 1880

Your Christ and Mine

To the artist He is the One Altogether Lovely.

To the architect He is the Chief Cornerstone.

To the baker He is the Living Bread.

To the builder He is the Sure Foundation.

To the doctor He is the Great Physician.

To the educator He is the Great Teacher.

To the farmer He is the Sower and the Lord of the Harvest.

To the florist He is the Lily of the Valley and the Rose of Sharon.

To the geologist He is the Rock of ages.

To the judge He is the Righteous Judge.

To the lawyer He is the Counsellor, the Lawgiver, and the Advocate.

To the newspaperman He is the Good Tidings of Great Joy.

To the philanthropist He is the Unspeakable Gift.

To the philosopher He is the Wisdom of God.

To the preacher He is the Word of God.

To the lonely He is the Friend that sticketh closer than a brother.

To the servant He is the Good Master.

cont'd.

It's All About Jesus

To the toiler He is the Giver of Rest.

To the seeker He is the Way, the Truth, and the Life.

To all who want to know . . . He is Jesus.

Author Unknown

Ken Blanchard

The grace of our Lord was poured out on me abundantly, along with the faith and love that are in Christ Jesus.

1 Timothy 1:14

Have you ever asked yourself, "What is life all about? Is there a purpose to what we are doing on this planet? Is there really a God that is personally concerned about me? And can I get to know Him?"

Well, I asked myself those questions for many years before I discovered the answers. I'm one of those individuals who came to know Jesus later in life.

But I'm getting ahead of myself. Let me take a moment and give you a little background on my journey.

I grew up in New Rochelle, New York. My parents attended church regularly and enjoyed their minister so much that they gave me his last name as my middle name, Kenneth 'Hartley' Blanchard.

I can't remember a time during my youth that we didn't go to church. It was there and in my home that the name of Jesus Christ was talked about. His name was very familiar and yet I did not really know him. You see, it's possible to know a lot about a person and still not know them. I know a great deal about President Abraham Lincoln but I never knew him on a personal basis.

In fact, I often heard the name of Jesus Christ outside of church activities. His was the most popular name on our school campus. And when I went into business I heard a good number of people talk about Jesus Christ. Of course, these individuals were using His name as a swear word.

After elementary school my parents moved the family to a new church that I attended throughout my junior high and high school years. The minister was a good speaker and very personable. It was there that I became very active in the Youth Fellowship. I especially enjoyed the new church because it had a great basketball team.

Although I enjoyed the sports activities, the church outings, and the relationships with other youth my age, I was still not a follower of Jesus. Church just seemed to be the normal way of life for our family. I really didn't give much thought to having a personal relationship with Jesus. It was more of a comfortable and casual acceptance that He was the Son of God. Sort of like believing in a historical event but having no emotions tied to it.

I then went off to college at Cornell University in Ithaca, in upstate New York. Under the university's hands-off policy with regard to student religious observances, I started to drift away. With studies and an increasingly busy campus life, I never really found a church to attend in Ithaca.

The summer after I graduated I started to date Margie McKee, who was a fourth generation Cornellian. We were both working in the Ithaca area. I was working as a dorm counselor for the National Science Foundation and playing a lot of golf. Margie was a speech therapy major. She worked at a special camp for handicapped kids. We were married a year later, after Margie's graduation from Cornell.

During our first year of marriage we lived in Hamilton, New York. I was finishing my master's degree and Margie was working as a speech therapist for the Madison County schools. When we returned to Cornell the next year for my doctorate and Margie for her master's degree, we met a fabulous young minister. He got us excited about church again. We even volunteered to help run the junior high program.

In 1966, we headed out to Ohio University in Athens for my first job as administrative assistant to the dean of the College of Business Administration. Our son, Scott, was just a baby, and Margie was pregnant with Debbie. In Athens, we met a wonderful minister and began to be active in that church.

This was the late sixties, a time of much student unrest. The

Kent State incident occurred right down the road. We had our own little incident of disillusionment that fit right in with the times. Our minister friend sympathized with students; he was right up front at all the protests and marches. That didn't go over well with his congregation. They fired him in what seemed to us a most un-Christian manner.

Anger and disillusionment came crashing in on us. We thought, *If that's what Christianity is all about, forget it.* We dropped out. Like so many people, if we went to church at all, it was only on Christmas and Easter. That went on for fifteen years.

In 1970, we moved to Amherst, Massachusetts where I taught at the University of Massachusetts and Margie worked on her doctorate in Communication Studies. After six years there, we went to San Diego for a one-year sabbatical leave. Living for a few months in California where sunshine is cheap, we realized that summer in Massachusetts, by comparison, was two weeks of bad skating. As a result, we decided to stay on the West Coast and start our own company, Blanchard Training and Development, Inc.

Then an unbelievably exciting event occurred: *The One Minute Manager*®. Spencer Johnson, my coauthor, and I met at a party in November of 1980. He was the co-author of a wonderful children's series called ValueTales. Margie met Spencer first. She hand-carried him over to me and said, "Why don't you two work on a children's book for managers? They won't read anything else."

Spencer was working on a one minute parenting book with a psychiatrist. When he explained his approach to parenting, I told him I had been teaching those kinds of things to managers for years. So I invited him to a seminar I was giving the following Monday in San Diego. He came and sat in the back of the room and laughed throughout the day. At the end of the seminar, he ran up to me and said, "Forget parenting! Let's go for managers." That was the birth of *The One Minute Manager*®.

It's All About Jesus

In 1982, William Morrow Publishers picked up our book and within two weeks it was on the New York Times bestseller list. It stayed on the list for the next three years.

Several months after the book came out, I got a call from Phil Hodges, a longtime friend from Cornell. He wanted to know if we could get together for a walk on the beach. He had turned his life over to Jesus Christ several years before and had been praying for me ever since. When we took our walk, Phil asked, "Ken, why do you think *The One Minute Manager*® is such a runaway bestseller? Do you think it's because you're a better writer than anyone else or that you're smarter than most people?"

I said, "I don't think that at all. I've thought a lot about it. The success of *The One Minute Manager*® is too unbelievable for me to take any credit. I think God is involved."

He grinned. "Thank God," he said, "I hoped you would have that attitude."

That meeting with Phil marked the renewal of my spiritual journey, which had begun when I was a little guy being taken to church by my parents. Afterward, he kept calling me, sending me things to read, and pushing me to think about my relationship with Jesus.

Next, Margie and I met Bob and Linda Buford. Bob was a member of the Young Presidents Organization (YPO) the group that had convinced Margie and me to stay in California and start our own company.

On the way to a YPO conference in Mexico City, we saw Bob and Linda between flights at the Dallas-Fort Worth Airport. When we got on the plane I discovered that Bob's seat was across the aisle from mine. During our chatting, I went to get something from my wallet and found, tucked away among the bills, a little booklet about Christianity called *The Four Spiritual Laws*, written by Bill Bright, founder of Campus Crusade for Christ. My friend Phil had given it to me to read. I didn't recall putting it in my wallet, but there it was.

I said, "Bob, this booklet is in my wallet for some reason. Maybe it means we should talk about Christianity. I have a few questions I'd like to ask you."

"I'll do my best, Ken," said Bob. "But remember, I'm only a layman."

So there in the sky we started going over the booklet together. The first spiritual law stated: "God loves you and offers a wonderful plan for your life."

I could buy that one all right, but the second law was where my questions started. It contended that we are all sinners. That had always bothered me for two reasons. First, I don't like labels. If you call somebody a "sinner" they really get their back up. Second, from my standpoint as a humanist, the concept of original sin was too negative. I'd always thought that people should be considered to have "original potentiality." That is, as human beings we have the potential to be either good or bad.

When I asked Bob about original sin he said, "Let me ask you a question, Ken. Do you think you're as good as God?"

"Of course not," I answered. "The concept of God has to do with perfection."

"Okay. On a scale of 1 to 100, let's give God 100. We'll give Mother Teresa 90, and an ax murderer 5. Ken, you're a decent sort of guy and are trying to help others, so I'll give you 75. Now the special thing about Christianity is that God sent Jesus to earth to make up the difference between you and 100."

That appealed to me. I'd never heard grace explained that way. Ask anybody "on a scale of 1 to 100, with 100 being perfection, where would you rate yourself?" Nobody would say 100. We all know that we fall short of perfection. This was a much better way to explain grace than calling people sinners.

"Before you get too excited," Bob continued, "Let me give you the whole story. A lot of people don't like the fact that the ax murderer gets the same shot at heaven as Mother Teresa, but that's what grace is all about. It's not about deeds; it's about faith. If you accept Jesus Christ as your Savior, no matter what your past has been, He rids you of your sins and this makes up the difference between you and 100."

For the rest of the flight I peppered Bob with questions. As we deplaned in Mexico City, Bob said, "I've got a friend I want you to meet who can answer your questions much better than I can. His name is Bill Hybels, and he's minister of one of the fastest-growing churches in the country. And another thing—he's speaking at this conference. If it's okay, I'm going to see to it that you guys have lunch together."

Bill and I did have lunch. I led off with the same question I'd asked Bob: "Why original sin? It's too negative."

Bill said, "Ken, let me explain the difference between Christianity and religion. The main difference is in how they're spelled. Religion is spelled 'do.' That means there are all kinds of things you must do to receive God's grace. The problem with religion and the 'do' philosophy is that most people quit because they never know when enough is enough. Suppose you do 2,500 good things in your life, and then you get to Judgment Day and the Lord says, 'That's not bad but you needed to do 3,000.'"

Bill went on to say, "Christianity is spelled 'done.' The Lord sent Jesus to earth to take care of it. You can't perform well enough or do enough good things to get into heaven. The only entry is by admitting you are a sinner (that is, falling short of a 100 in Bob's terms) and accepting Jesus as your Savior. He is the only one who can cleanse your past. You cannot do it yourself." Bill talked about a personal relationship with Jesus, something I had not experienced even in the days when I was active in church. "Not only can He save you, but He can become your guide and your friend. He can energize your life and transform it."

The simplicity of Bill's explanation hit me. I had attended church for years, but I had never heard the message of grace with such clarity and power. All my misgivings about original sin were stripped away. I wasn't a bad person; I just fell short of God's perfection and by accepting Jesus as my Savior I could be given grace. Then I could reach 100 and be right with the Lord through God's forgiveness of my imperfections.

When I asked Bill how I could accept grace, he said, "It's easy for a One Minute Manager®! All you have to do is bow your head and say, 'Lord, I can't save myself; I am a sinner. I fall short of 100. I accept Jesus Christ as my Savior and bridge between me and You. From this day forward I turn my life over to Him.'"

While I was excited and could feel the adrenaline pumping, I was reluctant to jump in with both feet. And Bill could sense it. I told him I was worried about a commitment to Jesus because I was afraid I wouldn't be able to follow through. "I'll fail," I said.

Bill took out a pen and wrote the words "commit" and "follow through" on a paper napkin. Then he said, "Please don't ever use those two words. Becoming a Christian is not about committing and following through. God knows you can't keep your commitment. God knows you can't follow through. Christianity is a matter of two different words: *receive* and *trust*. Romans 6:23 says, 'For the wages of sin is death, but the free gift of God is eternal life in Jesus Christ our Lord.'

"What is a gift?" Bill asked.

I said, "Something you receive."

"That's right," said Bill. "Salvation, regeneration, newness of life, and forgiveness of sin are things that can only be received. And once you receive grace, once you receive forgiveness, you've got them. Your next step is to trust God and say, 'I don't know what all of this means, and I don't know where I am going, but I am going to trust You each step of the way and see what happens.'"

My lunch with Bill really made me think about Jesus. But I still wasn't ready to suit up yet. I just wasn't ready to let go of my life and hand it over to God.

It's hard for human beings to let go completely. We think we can figure everything out for ourselves. I kept on thinking about what Bob and Bill had said, but it wasn't until almost a year later that I acknowledged I was seriously ready to suit up.

It occurred after Margie and I turned over the presidency of Blanchard Training and Development to an individual who had more business experience than we did and who felt he could move our company forward. As it turned out, we didn't always agree on some basic values. Margie and I tried everything to resolve this conflict, but no matter what we tried, it didn't help. It became clear that things were just not working out. What was worse, I felt powerless to do anything about it.

One evening, Margie and I decided to meet at a local restaurant for dinner and talk about our options.

Earlier that day, I recalled a conversation I'd had with Bill. We'd once talked about my work as a consultant, helping executives solve sticky problems that came up in their organizations. Bill had said, "Ken, I can't understand why you won't receive the gift of God's grace, because if you do, you get three top consultants for the price of one—the Father, who created it all; the Son, who taught us all we should know; and the Holy Spirit, who is our day-to-day operational manager. When you suit up for the Lord and accept Jesus as your Savior, the Holy Spirit jumps in and offers sure guidance whenever you're stuck. That's a good deal, Blanchard."

As my dinner meeting with Margie approached, I thought, *Man, why am I trying to solve this all by myself?* Suddenly, I knew what I was going to do. A wave of tremendous relief flowed through me. I bowed my head and said, *"Lord, I can't make it to 100 by myself. I can't solve problems like this without Your help. I admit that I need You and recognize my vulnerability. I accept Jesus as my Savior as the bridge between You and me."* The moment I said these words, a great peace came over me.

That feeling was still with me when I walked into the restaurant to meet Margie. She took one look at me and said, "What happened to you? You look so relaxed and calm." Then I told her what I had done and how I was going to trust God to give me the wisdom and strength to deal with the problem presented by our president. Later, I phoned Bill and left a message on his answering machine that I had received Christ and was ready to trust my life to Him.

My friend Phil told me one time that to appreciate Jesus and the gift God has given us, you have to recognize the differences between justice, mercy, and grace. With *justice,* if you commit a crime, you get the penalty you deserve. With *mercy,* if you commit a crime, you are given less punishment than you deserve. With *grace,* someone else has already taken the sentence—taken the punishment for you. The Lord loves us so much that He sacrificed His only son, Jesus, to wipe our slate clean and give us the gift of salvation.

You might be wondering what happened to Margie. Well she suited up a year later after reading Robert A. Laidlaw's *The Reason Why* during a ski trip to Aspen with a group of old Cornell friends.

The day before, she had hurt her leg skiing, so she decided to take it easy the rest of this trip. Phil gave Laidlaw's little booklet to Margie to read while the rest of us headed off to the slopes.

When I got back to the room at the end of our ski day, Margie said, "Well, I did it!"

I said, "Did what?"

"I suited up," she smiled. "Robert Laidlaw asked for a decision at the end of *The Reason Why*, so I bowed my head and did it."

Several years ago Charlie "Tremendous" Jones republished *The Reason Why* through Executive Books. Unbeknownst to me he asked Margie to write the foreword. I was touched when I read her comments:

> *Nearly ten years ago I spent a snowy afternoon reading* The Reason Why *while Ken and friends were skiing. Perhaps like you, I had both*

noticed and envied the deep joy I saw in people (like Ken) who had taken the promise of forgiveness of sins and eternal salvation into their hearts by accepting Jesus Christ as their personal Lord and Savior. It was a mystery to me. How did a person like me come to this decision and take what sounded like a simple but huge step?

The Reason Why *is 37 pages long. It very patiently goes through the intellectual questions you and I have about the existence of God, the Bible and the Word of God and, ultimately, God's offer and plan for our salvation and eternal life with Him.*

My beliefs, my faith, and my ego were all challenged in this little book as the case for God's wondrous and loving offer was built and rebuilt. At the end I was asked to leave my doubts behind, to rejoice in the invitation by God to take Jesus Christ into my heart as my personal savior, and to accept that offer period.

As I signed and dated this little book, I realized that faith is simply a choice – yes or no. Yes for me has made all the difference.

When Margie told me she had suited up after reading *The Reason Why*, I began to cry for two reasons. First, it reminded me of the impact Norman Vincent Peale had on our lives while I was writing *The Power of Ethical Management* with him in the late 1980's. Margie and I had not yet made a personal commitment to the Lord and Norman encouraged us by saying "The Lord has always had the two of you on his team, you just haven't 'suited up' yet." So "suiting up" became our faith mantra. Secondly, the fact that Margie suited up that day was special for her and for me. You suit up one at a time. Margie is not an emotional decision maker like I am. She is much more thoughtful. She had to suit up on her own time table. Now we are really on the same team—forever!

> *If we confess our sins, he is faithful and just and will forgive us our sins and purify us from all unrighteousness.*
>
> I John 1:9

Himself

Once it was the blessing, Now it is the Lord;
Once it was the feeling, Now it is His Word.
Once His gifts I wanted, Now the Giver own;
Once I sought for healing, Now Himself alone.

Once 'twas painful trying, Now 'tis perfect trust;
Once a half salvation, Now the uttermost.
Once 'twas ceaseless holding, Now He holds me fast;
Once 'twas constant drifting, Now my anchor's cast.

Once 'twas busy planning, Now 'tis trustful prayer;
Once 'twas anxious caring, Now He has the care.
Once 'twas what I wanted, Now what Jesus says;
Once 'twas constant asking, Now 'tis ceaseless praise.

Once it was my working, His it hence shall be;
Once I tried to use Him, Now He uses me.
Once the power I wanted, Now the Mighty One;
Once for self I labored, Now for Him alone.

Once I hoped in Jesus, Now I know He's mine;
Once my lamps were dying, Now they brightly shine.
Once for death I waited, Now His coming hail;
And my hopes are anchored, Safe within the veil.

Hymn by A. B. Simpson, 1904

I'd Rather Have Jesus

I'd rather have Jesus than silver or gold;
I'd rather be His than have riches untold;
I'd rather have Jesus than houses or lands;
I'd rather be led by His nail-pierced hand.

Than to be the king of a vast domain,
Or be held in sin's dread sway;
I'd rather have Jesus than anything
This world affords today.

I'd rather have Jesus than men's applause;
I'd rather be faithful to His dear cause;
I'd rather have Jesus than world-wide fame;
I'd rather be true to His holy name.

He's fairer than lilies of rarest bloom;
He's sweeter than honey from out the comb;
He's all that my hungering spirit needs;
I'd rather have Jesus and let Him lead.

Hymn by Rhea F. Miller, 1922

Part III
All Roads Lead to Jesus: How That Can Be True for You

Charles H. Spurgeon's Best Sermon

When asked which was the best sermon he ever preached, the noted nineteenth century British minister Charles Haddon Spurgeon responded: "My best sermon was the one which had the most love and the most Christ in it. One day," continued Spurgeon, "a young man preached a showy sermon before the great Jonathan Edwards, and when he had finished he asked Mr. Edwards what he thought of it.

"It was a very poor sermon indeed," said Edwards;

"A poor sermon!" said the young man, "It took me a long time to study for it."

"Ay, no doubt of it."

"Why, then do you say it was poor? Did you not think my explanation of the text to be accurate?"

"Oh, yes," said the old preacher, "Very correct indeed."

"Well, then, why do you say it was a poor sermon? Didn't you think the metaphors were appropriate, and the arguments conclusive?"

"Yes, they were very good, as far as that goes, but still it was a very poor sermon."

"Will you tell me why you think it was a poor sermon?"

"Because," said Edwards, "there was no Christ in it."

"Well," said the young man, "Christ was not in the text; we are not preaching Christ always, we must preach what is in the text."

"Then don't take a text without Christ in it. If you are careful you will find Christ in every text if you examine it. Don't you know, young man, that from every town, and every village, and every little hamlet in England, wherever it may be, there is a road that leads to London."

"Yes," said the young man.

"Ah!" said the old divine, "and so for every text in Scripture there is a road to the metropolis of the Scriptures, that leads to Christ. And, now dear brother, your business is, when you get to a text, to say, 'Now, what is the road to Christ?' and then preach a sermon, running along the road towards the great metropolis—Christ."

The old clergyman continued, "I have never yet found a text that had not a plain and direct road to Christ in it; and if ever I should find one that has no such road, I will make a road. I would go over hedge and ditch but I would get at my Master, for a sermon is neither fit for the Lord nor yet for the peasant unless there is a savor of Christ in it.

"You must continue to call upon Christ," said Spurgeon, "As the Turkish lady who fell in love with Thomas Becket's father called upon him.

"Becket's father, Gilbert, went to the Crusades, and was taken prisoner by the Saracens. While a prisoner this Turkish lady fell in love with him, and when he was set free and returned to England, she took an opportunity of escaping from her father's house.

"She boarded a ship, and came to England. But she did not know where to find the one she loved. All that she knew about him was that his name was Gilbert and he lived in England. She was determined to find him even if she had to go through all the streets of England, crying out the name of Gilbert, till she had found him.

"She went to London first. As she walked down every street, people were surprised to see an Eastern maiden, attired in an Eastern costume, crying, 'Gilbert! Gilbert! Gilbert!'

"And so she passed from town to town. Finally, one day she pronounced the name Gilbert and he heard it. She had found the one she loved and they were joined together.

"And so is the same today. The sinner may not have much knowledge of the Bible . . . but at least he knows the name of Jesus."

It's All About Jesus

"Take up the cry, sinner, and today, as you go along the streets, say in your heart, 'Jesus! Jesus! Jesus!' And when are in your own home, say it again 'Jesus! Jesus! Jesus!' Continue the cry, and it shall reach the ear for which it is meant."

Melville D. London
from *Kings of the Platform and Pulpit, 1896*

The Bible

"And the Word was made flesh and dwelt among us."

What book is that whose page divine
Bears God's impress on every line,
And in man's soul makes light to shine?
The Bible

When sin and sorrow, want and woe,
Assail poor mortals here below,
What book can then true comfort show?
The Bible

What paints the beautiful and true,
And mirrors at a single view
The paths which here we should pursue?
The Bible

What is the brightest gift the Lord
In his great mercy did award
To man, to be his shield and guard?
The Bible

What teaches love and truth and peace,
And bids good will among men increase?
And bids strife, war and murder cease?
The Bible

Oh! What can make this world of woe
With peace and truth and virtue glow,
Till men no sin nor sorrow know?
The Bible

cont'd.

It's All About Jesus

What gives to man the power and will,
God's high behest to do fulfill
And points the way to Zion's hill?
The Bible

When death comes knocking at the door,
And man's short life on earth is o'er,
What tells of bliss for ever more?
The Bible

Author Unknown

Spiritual Counseling and Your Soul

When it comes to spiritual counseling there seems to be three categories of people. With which category would you identify yourself?

1. The "Whatevers." There are those who couldn't care less about spiritual matters. They do not have any background in religious faith and do not feel a need to develop one. Or, if they do have some previous knowledge, they have chosen to reject it for various reasons.

2. The "Ah-has!" There are those who may or may not have some spiritual background, but are interested in the topic. They are seekers who are open to consider this avenue of life and would like further information.

3. The Thinkers. There are those who are deeply concerned about spiritual matters. Their emotional and mental health is tied closely to their faith and how it affects their daily lives. They strive, in various degrees, to attempt to grow in their faith and knowledge. Those who are interested or are deeply concerned about spiritual matters identify with the words of Jesus when he says: *"For what profit is it to a man if he gains the whole world, and loses his own soul? Or what will a man give in exchange for his soul?"* (Matthew 16:26).

Jesus is simply saying that there is more to life than just material goods. He suggests that it is dangerous to not consider the deeper purposes of life. Have you ever wondered what life is all about? Have you ever questioned why there is pain and suffering . . . and why there are headaches? Have you ever wondered if God has a plan for your life?

You see, life is not always an easy road. Sometimes we encounter the 'potholes' of difficulties, the pain of bumps, the detours of depression, and the roughness of headaches. During these times of discomfort, it is easy to become weary of it all. Are you tired and weary of the pressures in your life and the various troubles you face? Then join the club. Many people feel the same way.

Spiritual counseling suggests that God does care about you and the problems you face. God wants to come to your aid and help you through the tough times.

Jesus said, *"Come to Me, all you who labor and are heavy laden, and I will give you rest. Take My yoke upon you and learn from Me, for I am gentle and lowly in heart, and you will find rest for your souls. For My yoke is easy and My burden is light"* (Matthew 1:28-30).

How does one come to Jesus? How does a person find rest for their soul? How can I experience peace in the midst of turmoil? Jesus said, *"Peace I leave with you, My peace I give to you; not as the world gives do I give to you. Let not your heat be troubled, neither let it be afraid.* [John 14:27]

Perhaps you've been reading this book and you realize that you want your life to be all about Jesus, but don't know what to do. Read on, and I'll walk you through the steps.

In order to experience peace *with* God, and the peace *of* God, you have to start by understanding who Jesus is. He is God in a human body. He has come to tell us how to have a relationship with him that will last for eternity.

When we were in Mongolia, a professor of literature who was a Parliament Member said to me: *"I don't understand your God. He has three faces—Father, Son, and Holy Spirit. How can that be?"* The conversation followed:

"You are a professor of literature, are you not?"

"Yes, I am."

"Is the name Shakespeare familiar to you?"

"Of course."

"Are you acquainted with the character Macbeth?"

"Yes, I am."

"May I ask you a question? Could the character Macbeth ever meet the author, Shakespeare?

He thought for a moment and replied:

"No, he could not."

"Ahhh, but he could. All the author would have to do is to write himself into the play and then introduce himself to Macbeth. That's what God [the Father] did when he wrote himself into the play of life in the form of the Son [Jesus of Nazareth]. He became the God/man."

God is a perfect and holy being. We as humans are not perfect. We are not holy. We have imperfections. Try as we may, we often fall short of doing the right thing, saying the right thing, or thinking the right thing. Do you know anyone who is perfect?

This imperfection or sin is what separates us from a holy God. Now God has a problem. He loves us but must also deal with our sinfulness—our imperfections. His Son was sent to die in our place . . . pay our penalty . . . and to buy us back from the slave market of sinfulness and wickedness.

Jesus bore our sins on the cross for us. He died in our place. He was buried for our cruelty. And He rose from the grave to establish a new life and relationship with God for us. All we have to do is to have faith in this event.

The Apostle Paul states it this way, *"That if you confess with your mouth the Lord Jesus and believe in your heart that God has raised Him from the dead, you will be saved. For with the heart one believes unto righteousness, and with the mouth confession is made unto salvation . . . For whoever calls on the name of the Lord shall be saved* (Romans 10:9-10, 13).

Have you ever done that before? If not, you can do it right now. Just put down this book and pray a simple prayer of faith asking Jesus to come into your life. Thank him for dying in your place. Thank him for providing a new relationship with God.

Ask God to bring people into your life who can help you to grow and to learn more about Him. Thank Him for saving you.

When someone invites Jesus to come into his or her life, God sends His Holy Spirit to dwell within. He will be there to teach you about God. He will support you in tough times. He will help you to endure pain and suffering, and He will teach and lead you to learn more about Him.

To encourage you in the decision you just made, I would suggest that you read the following verses from the Bible and then write what you learned from them in the space provided:

> Revelation 3:20, *Here I am! I stand at the door and knock. If anyone hears my voice and opens the door, I will come in and eat with him, and he with me.*

> Colossians 1:14, 27 *in whom we have redemption, the forgiveness of sins. To them God has chosen to make known among the Gentiles the glorious riches of this mystery, which is Christ in you, the hope of glory.*

> I John 5:11-13 *And this is the testimony: God has given us eternal life, and this life is in his Son. He who has the Son has life; he who does not have the Son of God does not have life. I write these things to you who believe in the name of the Son of God so that you may know that you have eternal life.*

> John 6:37 *All that the Father gives me will come to me, and whoever comes to me I will never drive away.*

> Romans 10:9-13 *That if you confess with your*

mouth, "Jesus is Lord," and believe in your heart that God raised him from the dead, you will be saved. For it is with your heart that you believe and are justified, and it is with your mouth that you confess and are saved. As the Scripture says, "Anyone who trusts in him will never be put to shame." For there is no difference between Jew and Gentile—the same Lord is Lord of all and richly blesses all who call on him, for, "Everyone who calls on the name of the Lord will be saved."

Hebrews 13:5 *Keep your lives free from the love of money and be content with what you have, because God has said, "Never will I leave you; never will I forsake you."*

What did you learn from these verses?

____

____

____

____

Read the Bible every day. Following is a very simple daily Bible study plan.

A. Select one of the books within the Bible that you would like to read. A good book to start with would be the fourth book in the New Testament called the Gospel of John.

B. Read one chapter a day until you are finished with that book.

C. As you read each chapter make some notes. Try and identify the following:

1. The key verse of the chapter (The central thought).
2. God's commands (A command is something to do).
3. God's promises (A promise is something to be believed).
4. A short summary of the chapter.
5. Personal applications that you received from reading that particular chapter that you can apply to your daily life.

D. Read I Peter 2:2 *Like newborn babies, crave pure spiritual milk, so that by it you may grow up in your salvation* and Psalm 119:9,11 *How can a young man keep his way pure? By living according to your word. I have hidden your word in my heart that I might not sin against you.*

Talk to God daily (prayer) and keep your relationship with Him growing.

Read I John 1:9 *If we confess our sins, he is faithful and just and will forgive us our sins and purify us from all unrighteousness.*

Psalm 66:18 *If I had cherished sin in my heart, the Lord would not have listened.*

Philippians 4:6-7 *Do not be anxious about anything, but in everything, by prayer and petition, with thanksgiving, present your requests to God. And the peace of God, which transcends all understanding, will guard your hearts and your minds in Christ Jesus.*

Fellowship with other believers. Get involved in a local church where the truth about Jesus is taught. In Hebrews 10:25 we read *Let us not give up meeting together, as some are in the habit of doing, but let us encourage one another—and all the more as you see the Day approaching.*

Begin to tell others about Jesus. Learn to serve God wherever you can. Help others grow in their faith. Read

Matthew 28:19-20 *Therefore go and make disciples of all nations, baptizing them in the name of the Father and of the Son and of the Holy Spirit, and teaching them to obey everything I have commanded you. And surely I am with you always, to the very end of the age.*

Mark 5:19 *Jesus did not let him, but said, "Go home to your family and tell them how much the Lord has done for you, and how he has had mercy on you."*

Acts 1:8 *But you will receive power when the Holy Spirit comes on you; and you will be my witnesses in Jerusalem, and in all Judea and Samaria, and to the ends of the earth.*

Ephesians 4:29 *Do not let any unwholesome talk come out of your mouths, but only what is helpful for building others up according to their needs, that it may benefit those who listen.*

I Corinthians 10:31 *So whether you eat or drink or whatever you do, do it all for the glory of God.*

What did you learn from reading these Bible verses?

____

____

____

____

To help you to grow in the spiritual realm we have included Bible study helps for various life topics. They can be found at the back of the book. May your soul be refreshed as you study the Word of God.

The Westminster Confession of Faith Regarding Jesus

I. **It pleased God,** in His eternal purpose, to choose and ordain the Lord Jesus, His only begotten Son, to be the Mediator between God and man, the Prophet, Priest, and King, the Head and Savior of His Church, the Heir of all things, and Judge of the world: unto whom He did from all eternity give a people, to be His seed, and to be by Him in time redeemed, called, justified, sanctified, and glorified.

II. **The Son of God,** the second person in the Trinity, being very and eternal God, of one substance and equal with the Father, did, when the fullness of time was come, take upon Him man's nature, with all the essential properties and common infirmities thereof, yet without sin; being conceived by the power of the Holy Ghost, in the womb of the virgin Mary, of her substance. So that two whole, perfect, and distinct natures, the Godhead and the manhood, were inseparably joined together in one person, without conversion, composition, or confusion. Which person is very God, and very man, yet one Christ, the only Mediator between God and man.

III. **The Lord Jesus,** in His human nature thus united to the divine, was sanctified, and anointed with the Holy Spirit, above measure, having in Him all the treasures of wisdom and knowledge, in whom it pleased the Father that all fullness should dwell; to the end that, being holy, harmless, undefiled, and full of grace and truth, He might be thoroughly furnished to execute the office of a Mediator and Surety. Which office He took not unto Himself, but was thereunto called by His Father, who put all power and judgment into His hand, and gave Him commandment to execute the same.

IV. **This office the Lord Jesus** did most willingly undertake; which that He might discharge, He was made under the law, and did perfectly fulfill it; endured most grievous torments immediately in His soul, and most painful sufferings in His body; was crucified, and died, was buried, and remained under the power of death, yet saw no corruption. On the third day He arose from the dead, with the same body in which He suffered, with which also He ascended into heaven, and there sitteth at the right hand of His Father, making intercession, and shall return, to judge men and angels, at the end of the world.

V. **The Lord Jesus,** by His perfect obedience, and sacrifice of Himself, which He through the eternal Spirit, once offered up unto God, hath fully satisfied the justice of His Father; and purchased, not only reconciliation, but an everlasting inheritance in the kingdom of heaven, for all those whom the Father hath given unto Him.

VI. **Although the work of redemption** was not actually wrought by Christ till after His incarnation, yet the virtue, efficacy, and benefits thereof are communicated unto the elect, in all ages successively from the beginning of the world, in and by those promises, types, and sacrifices, wherein He was revealed, and signified to be the seed of the woman which should bruise the serpent's head; and the Lamb slain from the beginning of the world; being yesterday and today the same, and forever.

VII. **Christ, in the work of mediation,** acts according to both natures, by each nature doing that which is proper to itself; yet, by reason of the unity of the person, that which is proper to one nature is sometimes in Scripture attributed to the person dominated by the other nature.

VIII. **To all those for whom Christ** hath purchased redemption, He doth certainly and effectually apply and communicate the same; making intercession for them, and revealing unto them, and in and by the Word, the mysteries of salvation; effectually persuading them by His Spirit to believe and obey, and governing their hearts by His Word and Spirit; overcoming all their enemies by His almighty power and wisdom, in such manner, and ways, as are most consonant to His wonderful and unsearchable dispensation.

American Revision of the
Westminster Confession of Faith
Regarding Jesus, 1787-89

Part IV
Learning More About Jesus

Studies in the Life of Christ

Anyone who studies human history cannot ignore Jesus. All of ancient history converges at His cross. All of time circles around Him as either BC or AD. Jesus can be no more expelled from human history than the sun can be expelled from the sky.

No one in all of history or philosophy has ever spoken or lived like Jesus. The believer and the non-believer both must acknowledge Him and bow to His wisdom, His holiness, and His love for others. Many people have proudly claimed, "I'm an atheist. I do not believe in God." Others have said, "I'm an agnostic. No one can know if there is a God or not." Did you know that the word 'agnostic' comes from the Latin word 'ignoramus?' An ignoramus is an ignorant person, a dunce.

Throughout history millions of people have claimed to have had their lives changed by a personal encounter with Jesus. They may say things like:

- "I was an alcoholic. Jesus came into my life and He has set me free from drink."
- "I was hooked on drugs, but Jesus changed my life. I no longer do drugs."
- "I was depressed and ready to commit suicide until I met Jesus. He has given me peace and a purpose for living."
- "I had a hard time forgiving those who had hurt me until I met Jesus. Then I realized that I had hurt Him by my sinful lifestyle, yet He forgave me. I can now also forgive others."
- "I've had tremendous success and made a lot of money. I started to think I was a big deal and then I met Jesus. I realized that accumulating earthly wealth is not really important and my ego had gotten out of control. He straightened out my life and now I seek first the Kingdom of God.

When was the last time you heard an atheist or agnostic say:

- "I was an alcoholic. Since I started believing in atheism I've been set free from drink."
- "I was hooked on drugs, but atheism changed my life. I no longer do drugs."
- "I was depressed and ready to commit suicide until I became an agnostic. Agnosticism has given me peace and a purpose for living."
- "I had a hard time forgiving those who had hurt me until I became an agnostic. My agnosticism helps me to forgive others."

You will probably have to wait for a long, *long* time before you will hear about changed lives because of atheism or agnosticism. All other religions of the world seek after God, or seek to find some kind of peace through a belief or a secret philosophy of living. It's only in Christianity where God seeks after humankind.

The more you study the life of Jesus, the more you will understand that "God so loved the world that he gave his one and only Son, that whoever believes in him shall not perish but have everlasting life." (John 3:16)

It has been said that the only things that are sure are death and taxes. We're all going to have to face death at one time or another. Then what? Is there life after death? G.B. Hardy once stated that there are only two important questions in life. The first is, "Has anyone ever cheated death and lived to prove it?" And the second is, "Is it available to me?"

He went on to say, "Let's look at the record. Buddha's tomb—occupied. Mohammad's tomb—occupied. Confucius' tomb—occupied. Jesus' tomb—empty." He then said, "Argue as you will . . . there's no point in following a loser."

Being a Christian is more than just an instantaneous conversion; it is like a daily process whereby you grow to be more and more like Christ.

Billy Graham

Jesus: The Greatest Leadership Role Model of All Time

My first realization that Jesus was the greatest leadership role model of all time came as a result of *The One Minute Manager®*. Part of that success got me invited to be on television and radio programs all over the country. One of the most exciting invitations was to be interviewed by Dr. Robert Schuller on *The Hour of Power*, televised from the Chrystal Cathedral. Dr. Schuller loved *The One Minute Manager* and what he said about it began a process that is continuing to change my life forever. Dr. Schuller suggested that Jesus was a classic One Minute Manager. When I asked him to explain why, he was very clear. As I recall the conversation, Dr. Schuller says, "First, Jesus was very clear on goals, and isn't the first secret of being a One Minute Manager called one-minute goal setting?" I certainly had to agree with that. Then Dr. Schuller smiled and said, "Tom Peters and you did not invent 'management by walking around' – Jesus did! He wandered from one village to another, always looking to see if He could catch someone doing something right. When people showed signs of believing Him and the good news He brought, Jesus would heal them, praise them and encourage them. Isn't the second secret of the One Minute Manager referred to as a One Minute Praising?"

Finally Dr. Schuller implied that if people were off base, Jesus wasn't afraid to redirect them or chastise them as he did with the money lenders in the church. And that was appropriate. "After all, the final secret of the One Minute Manager is the one minute reprimand."

Robert Schuller's comments about Jesus as a One Minute Manager got me thinking. As I began to deepen in my faith and delve into the Bible, and as a behavioral scientist, I went straight to the Gospels – Matthew, Mark, Luke and John – and the book of Acts because I wanted to know what Jesus did. As I studied those books, I became fascinated with how Jesus transformed twelve ordinary and unlikely people into the first generation of leaders of a movement that continues to affect the course of history some two thousand years later. I soon became aware that everything I had ever taught or written about Jesus did to perfection, beyond my ability to portray or describe. After studying leadership for more than thirty years, I came to the conclusion that Jesus is the greatest leadership role model of all time. And do we ever need a different leadership role model today! I realized that Christians have more in Jesus than just a spiritual leader; they have a practical and effective leadership model for all organizations, for all people, for all situations.

Today, in the headlines we read about corporate America leaders who exploit privileges of position bringing ruin to employees and investors. Meanwhile, citizens of underdeveloped countries languish in poverty and hopelessness in a leadership vacuum. At the same time all across the country, the witness and ministry of a number of churches have been compromised and stymied by a crisis of integrity in their leaders. In stark contrast to these failures and foibles of twenty-first century leadership stands the perfect leadership role model – Jesus of Nazareth.

As a result of this insight and the realization that few, if any, divinity schools or pastors were teaching about Jesus as a great leadership role model, in 1999 I co-founded with Phil Hodges the Center for Faithwalk Leadership. The initial intent of the Center was to help people walk their faith in the marketplace. The center was started after Phil and I began working on *Leadership by the Book* with Bill Hybels.

When we started the Center, we began training people to be servant leaders as Jesus had mandated. We are convinced that

Jesus calls all who follow Him to become His leadership disciples. He was very clear and emphatic in His instructions that His followers were to be like servants when John and James seemed to be vying for a special leadership role among the disciples.

> *Jesus called them together and said, "You know that the rulers of the Gentiles lord it over them, and their high officials exercise authority over them. Not so with you. Instead, whoever wants to become great among you must be your servant, and whoever wants to be first must be your slave—just as the Son of Man did not come to be served, but to serve, and to give his life as a ransom for many."*
>
> Matthew 20:25-28

The key phrase is "not so with you." That Jesus called us to a way of leading born out of service and obedience is clear and unequivocal. No plan B is implied or offered. No restrictions or limitations to only religious leadership are made or inferred. For Christian leaders this is not a suggestion, it is a mandate.

Today, with the help of Greg Bunch, a member of the Center's national board, and folks he works with at Brand Trust in Chicago—the Center for Faithwalk Leadership is our address at best. They helped Phil, Phyllis Hendry, our ministry president, and me realize that our purpose is to glorify God by inspiring and equipping people to lead like Jesus. We are in the Lead Like Jesus business. We now call our ministry a movement because our hope is that someday 6.8 billion souls will be impacted by someone who leads like Jesus. We imagine a world in which leaders serve rather than rule, a world in which they give rather than take. We imagine leaders who seek to produce results and services. We recognize that this only happens as leaders adopt Jesus as their leadership role model and grow in His likeness.

Since I'm not retiring but re-firing, my goal is to take the message of Lead Like Jesus all over the world. People who hear about us can go to our website, www.LeadLikeJesus.com and learn what a fabulous boss I am working for now.

Ken Blanchard

Why Did Jesus Come?

Jesus came to save us from everlasting separation from God. Jesus came to give us eternal life. Take a moment and soak in what the Bible has to say about Jesus saving us from the penalty of our sinful nature:

> *And everyone who calls on the name of the Lord will be saved.*
>
> Acts 2:21 NIV

> *It is by the name of Jesus Christ of Nazareth, whom you crucified but whom God raised from the dead, that this man stands before you healed. He is "'the stone you builders rejected, which has become the capstone.' Salvation is found in no one else, for there is no other name under heaven given to men by which we must be saved."*
>
> Acts 4:10-12 NIV

> *The jailer called for lights, rushed in and fell trembling before Paul and Silas. He then brought them out and asked, "Sirs, what must I do to be saved?" They replied, "Believe in the Lord Jesus, and you will be saved—you and your household."*
>
> Acts 16:29-31 NIV

> *Since we have now been justified by his blood, how much more shall we be saved from God's wrath through him! For if, when we were God's enemies, we were reconciled to him through the death of his Son, how much more, having been reconciled, shall we be saved*

through his life! Not only is this so, but we also rejoice in God through our Lord Jesus Christ, through whom we have now received reconciliation.

Romans 5:9-11 NIV

"The word is near you; it is in your mouth and in your heart," that is, the word of faith we are proclaiming: That if you confess with your mouth, "Jesus is Lord," and believe in your heart that God raised him from the dead, you will be saved. For it is with your heart that you believe and are justified, and it is with your mouth that you confess and are saved. As the Scripture says, "Anyone who trusts in him will never be put to shame." For there is no difference between Jew and Gentile—the same Lord is Lord of all and richly blesses all who call on him, for, "Everyone who calls on the name of the Lord will be saved."

Romans 10:8-13 NIV

For the message of the cross is foolishness to those who are perishing, but to us who are being saved it is the power of God.

1 Corinthians 1:18 NIV

But thanks be to God, who always leads us in triumphal procession in Christ and through us spreads everywhere the fragrance of the knowledge of him. For we are to God the aroma of Christ among those who are being saved and those who are perishing. To the one we are the smell of death; to the other, the fragrance of life.

2 Corinthians 2:14-16 NIV

But because of his great love for us, God, who is rich in mercy, made us alive with Christ even when we were dead in transgressions—it is by grace you have been saved. And God raised us up with Christ and seated us with him in the heavenly realms in Christ Jesus, in order that in the coming ages he might show the incomparable riches of his grace, expressed in his kindness to us in Christ Jesus. For it is by grace you have been saved, through faith—and this not from yourselves, it is the gift of God—not by works, so that no one can boast. For we are God's workmanship, created in Christ Jesus to do good works, which God prepared in advance for us to do.

Ephesians 2:4-10 NIV

I urge, then, first of all, that requests, prayers, intercession and thanksgiving be made for everyone—for kings and all those in authority, that we may live peaceful and quiet lives in all godliness and holiness. This is good, and pleases God our Savior, who wants all men to be saved and to come to a knowledge of the truth. For there is one God and one mediator between God and men, the man Christ Jesus, who gave Himself as a ransom for all men—the testimony given in its proper time.

1 Timothy 2:1-6 NIV

But when the kindness and love of God our Savior appeared, he saved us, not because of righteous things we had done, but because of his mercy. He saved us through the washing of rebirth and renewal by the Holy Spirit, whom he poured out on us generously through Jesus Christ our Savior, so that, having been justified by his grace, we might become heirs having the hope of eternal life.

Titus 3:4-7 NIV

But don't forget this, dear friends, that a day or a thousand years from now is like tomorrow to the Lord. He isn't really being slow about his promised return, even though it sometimes seems that way. But he is waiting, for the good reason that he is not willing that any should perish, and he is giving more time for sinners to repent.

Dear friends, while you are waiting for these things to happen and for him to come, try hard to live without sinning; and be at peace with everyone so that he will be pleased with you when he returns.

And remember why he is waiting. He is giving us time to get his message of salvation out to others.

2 Peter 3:8-10, 14-15 TLB

On the following pages you will find various Bible studies about Jesus. They have been placed there to help expand your knowledge about the Savior. Our prayer is that you will be encouraged, challenged, and will be drawn closer to Jesus as you learn of him.

The Christ of the Bible

More than 1,900 years ago there was a Man born contrary to the laws of life. This Man lived in poverty and was reared in obscurity. He did not travel extensively. Only once did He cross the boundary of the country in which He lived and that was during His exile in childhood.

He possessed neither name, wealth, nor influence. His relatives were inconspicuous, uninfluential, and had neither training nor education.

In infancy He startled a king; in childhood He puzzled the doctors; in manhood He ruled the course of nature, walked upon billows as if pavements, and hushed the sea to sleep.

He healed the multitudes without medicine and made no charge for His service.

He never wrote a book, and yet all the libraries of the country could not hold the books that have been written about Him.

He never wrote a song, and yet He has furnished the theme for more songs than all the songwriters combined.

He never founded a college, but all the schools put together cannot boast of having as many students.

He never practiced medicine, and yet He has healed more broken hearts than all the doctors far and near.

He never marshaled an army, nor drafted a soldier, nor fired a gun, and yet no leader ever had more volunteers who have, under His orders, made more rebels stack arms and surrender without a shot being fired.

He is the Star of astronomy, the Rock of geology, the Lion and Lamb of the zoological kingdom.

He is the Revealer of the snares that lurk in the darkness; the Rebuker of every evil thing that prowls by night; the Quickener of all that is wholesome; the Adorner of all that is beautiful; the Reconciler of all that is contradictory; the Harmonizer of all discords; the Healer of all diseases; and the Savior of all mankind.

He fills the pages of theology and hymnology. Every prayer that goes up to God goes up in His name and is asked to be granted for His sake.

Every seventh day the wheels of commerce cease their turning and multitudes wend their way to worshiping assemblies to pay homage and respect to Him.

The names of the past proud statesmen of Greece and Rome have come and gone. The names of the past scientists, philosophers, and theologians have come and gone; but the name of this Man abounds more and more. Though time has spread 1,900 years between the people of this generation and the scene of His crucifixion, yet He still lives. Herod could not kill Him. Satan could not seduce Him. Death could not hold Him.

He stands forth upon the highest pinnacle of heavenly glory, proclaimed of God, acknowledged by angels, adored by saints, and feared by devils, as the living, personal Christ.

This Man, as you know, is Jesus Christ, our Lord and Savior!

A study of the Bible reveals Christ as its central subject and great theme. What the hub is to the wheel, Christ is to the Bible. It revolves around Him. All its types point to Him, and all its truths converge in Him. All its glories reflect Him, all its promises radiate from Him, all its beauties are embodied by Him, all its demands are exemplified by Him, and all its predictions are accepted by Him.

Abel's lamb was a type of Christ. Abraham offering Isaac on Mount Moriah was a type of God giving Christ, His only Son, on Mount Calvary. The Passover lamb in Egypt was a type of Christ—He told Nicodemus so Himself. The scapegoat typified Him bearing our sins. The scarlet thread that the harlot Rahab hung in the window of her home in Jericho typified Him. Joseph, pictured to us by the Bible without a flaw, was a type of Christ "who did not sin, neither was guile found in his mouth."

In the Old Testament He is spoken of as "the angel of the Lord," and as such He appeared unto men.

He was with Adam and Eve in the Garden of Eden. He was with Abel in his death. He walked with Enoch. He rode with Noah in the Ark. He ate with Abraham in his desert tent. He pled with Lot to leave wicked Sodom.

He watched Isaac reopen the wells that his father Abraham had dug. He wrestled with Jacob at Peniel. He strengthened Joseph in his time of temptation, protected him in prison, and exalted him to first place in the kingdom. He watched over Moses in the ark of bulrushes, talked to him from the burning bush, went down into Egypt with him, opened the Red Sea for him, fed him on bread from heaven, protected him with a pillar of fire by night, and after 120 years of such blessed companionship that they left no marks of passing time upon Moses, led him up from the plains of Moab unto the mountain of Nebo, to the top of Pisgah, let him take one long, loving look at the Promised Land, and then kissed him to sleep, folded Moses' hands over his breast, and buried his body in an unmarked grave, to sleep in Jesus till the morning of the great resurrection day.

He was the Captain of the Lord's host to Joshua, led him over the swollen stream of Jordan in flood tide, around Jericho, in conquest of Ai, helped him conquer Canaan, divide the land, and say good-bye to the children of Israel. He was with Gideon and his famous 300. He was with Samuel when he rebuked Saul. He was with David when he wrote the twenty-third psalm and slew the giant Goliath. He was with Solomon when he built the first temple. He was with good king Hezekiah when Sennacherib invaded the land. He was with Josiah in his great reformation that brought the people back to the law. He was with Ezekiel and Daniel in Babylon. He was with Jeremiah in Egypt. He was with Ezra when he returned from Babylon, and with Nehemiah when he rebuilt the wall. In fact, He was with all those "who through faith subdued kingdoms, wrought righteousness, obtained promises, stopped the mouths of lions, quenched the violence of fire, escaped the edge of the sword, out of weakness were made strong, waxed valiant in fight, turned to flight the armies of the aliens."

Abraham saw His day and rejoiced. Jacob called Him the "Lawgiver of Judah." Moses called Him the "Prophet that was to come." Job called Him "My Living Redeemer." Daniel called Him the "Ancient of Days." Jeremiah called him "The Lord our Righteousness." Isaiah called Him "Wonderful Counselor, the Mighty God, the Everlasting Father, the Prince of Peace."

All of this in the Old Testament? Yes, and much more besides. "To Him give all the prophets witness." Micah tells of the place of His birth. Jonah tells of His death, burial, and resurrection. Amos tells of His second coming to build again the tabernacles of David. Joel describes the day of His wrath. Zechariah tells of His coming reign as King over all the earth. Ezekiel gives us a picture of His millennial temple.

In fact, my friends, it matters little where we wander down the aisles, avenues, byways, or highways of the Old Testament. Jesus walks beside us as He walked beside the two disciples on that dusty road to Emmaus on that glorious resurrection day long, long ago.

Its types tell of Him, its sacrifices show Him, its symbols signify Him, its histories are His-stories, its songs are His sentiments, its prophecies are His pictures, its promises are His pledges; and our hearts burn within us as we walk beside Him across its living pages!

When we open the New Testament, the Word which was in the beginning with God becomes flesh and dwells among us, and we behold His glory, the glory as of the only begotten of the Father, full of grace and truth.

There are four personal histories of His earthly life written in the New Testament. One is by Matthew, the redeemed publican, and signifies His lineage; one is by Mark, the unknown servant, which magnifies His service; one is by Luke, "the beloved physician," and tells of His humanity; and one is by John, "whom Jesus loved," and it tells of His deity. He is Christ the King in Matthew, the Servant in Mark, the Man in Luke, and the Incarnate Word in John.

Concerning His royal lineage we learn that He was born in Bethlehem, the Seed of Abraham, the Son of David, the Son of Mary, the Son of God; and was acknowledged as "King of the Jews," "Christ the Lord," "God's Son," "The Savior of Men," by angels, demons, shepherds, and wise men; and that He received tributes of gold, frankincense, and myrrh.

Concerning His service we learn that He labored as a carpenter, opened eyes of the blind, unstopped deaf ears, loosed dumb tongues, cleansed lepers, healed the sick, restored withered hands, fed the hungry, sympathized with the sad, washed the disciple's feet, wept with Mary and Martha, preached the Gospel to the poor, went about doing good, and gave His life as a ransom for many.

Concerning His humanity we learn that He was born of a woman, as a little babe was wrapped in swaddling clothes, grew up and developed as a child in wisdom, stature, and in favor with God and men. He worked with His hands, He grew weary, He hungered, He thirsted, He slept, He felt the surge of anger; knew what it was to be sad, shed tears, sweat drops of blood; was betrayed, went through the mockery of a criminal trial, was scourged, had His hands and feet pierced; wore a crown of thorns, was spit upon, was crucified, was wrapped in a winding sheet, and was buried in a borrowed tomb behind a sealed stone, and was guarded by Roman soldiers in His death.

Concerning His deity we read that He was born of a virgin, lived a sinless life, spoke matchless words, stilled storms, calmed waves, rebuked winds, multiplied loaves, turned water into wine, raised the dead, foretold the future, gave hearing to the deaf, sight to the blind, speech to the dumb, cast out demons, healed diseases, forgave sins, claimed equality with

God, arose from the dead, and possessed all authority both in heaven and in earth.

He was both God and Man; two individuals united in one personality. "As man, He thirsted; as God, He gave living water. As man, He went to a wedding; as God, He turned the water to wine. As man, He slept in a boat; as God He stilled the storm. As man, He was tempted; as God He sinned not. As man, He wept; as God, He raised Lazarus from the dead. As man, He prayed; as God, He makes intercession for all men."

This is what Paul means when he writes, "Without controversy great is the mystery of godliness; God was manifest in the flesh, justified in the Spirit, seen of angels, preached unto the Gentiles, believed on in the world, received up into glory." He was made unto us wisdom, righteousness, sanctification, and redemption. He is the Light of the world. He is the Bread of Life. He is the True Vine. He is the Good Shepherd. He is the Way. He is the Life. He is the Door to Heaven.

He is the Faithful Witness, the First Begotten of the dead, the Prince of the kings of the earth, the King of kings, and the Lord of lords, Alpha and Omega, the first and the last, the beginning and the end, the Lord who is, who was, and who is to come, the Almighty. "I am He that liveth, and was dead; and behold, I am alive forevermore, and I have the keys of hell and of death."

He is the theme of the Bible from beginning to end: He is my Savior, let Him be your Savior, too!

In Genesis He is the Seed of the Woman

In Exodus He is the Passover Lamb

In Leviticus He is our High Priest

In Numbers He is the Pillar of Cloud by day and the Pillar of Fire by night.

In Deuteronomy He is the Prophet like unto Moses

It's All About Jesus

In Joshua He is the Captain of our Salvation

In Judges He is our Judge and Lawgiver

In Ruth He is our Kinsman Redeemer

In 1st and 2nd Samuel He is our Trusted Prophet

In Kings and Chronicles He is our Reigning King

In Ezra He is the Rebuilder of the broken-down walls of human life

In Esther He is our Mordecai

In Job He is our Ever-Living Redeemer, "For I know my redeemer liveth."

In Psalms He is our Shepherd

In Proverbs and Ecclesiastes He is our Wisdom

In the Song of Solomon He is our Lover and Bridegroom

In Isaiah He is the Prince of Peace

In Jeremiah He is the Righteous Branch

In Lamentations He is our Weeping Prophet

In Ezekiel He is the wonderful Four-Faced Man

In Daniel the Fourth Man in "Life's Fiery Furnaces"

In Hosea He is the Faithful Husband, "Forever married to the backslider."

In Joel He is the Baptizer with the Holy Ghost and Fire

In Amos He is our Burden-Bearer

In Obadiah He is the Mighty to Save

It's All About Jesus

In Jonah He is our great Foreign Missionary

In Micah He is the Messenger of Beautiful Feet

In Nahum He is the Avenger of God's Elect

In Habakkuk He is God's Evangelist, crying, "Revive thy work in the midst of the years."

In Zephaniah He is our Savior

In Haggai He is the Restorer of God's lost heritage

In Zechariah He is the Fountain opened to the house of David for sin and uncleanness

In Malachi He is the Sun of Righteousness, rising with healing in His wings

In Matthew He is the Messiah

In Mark He is the Wonder-Worker

In Luke He is the Son of Man

In John He is the Son of God

In Acts He is the Holy Ghost

In Romans He is our Justifier

In 1st and 2nd Corinthians He is our Sanctifier

In Galatians He is our Redeemer from the curse of the law

In Ephesians He is the Christ of unsearchable riches

In Philippians He is the God who supplies all our needs

In Colossians He is the fullness of the Godhead, bodily

In 1st and 2nd Thessalonians He is our Soon-Coming King

In 1st and 2nd Timothy He is our Mediator between God and man

In Titus He is our Faithful Pastor

In Philemon He is a Friend that sticketh closer than a brother

In Hebrews He is the Blood of the Everlasting Covenant

In James He is our Great Physician, for "The prayer of faith shall save the sick."

In 1st and 2nd Peter He is our Chief Shepherd, who soon shall appear with a crown of unfading glory

In 1st, 2nd, and 3rd John He is Love

In Jude He is the Lord coming with ten thousands of His saints

In Revelation He is the King of kings and Lord of lords!

He is Abel's Sacrifice, Noah's Rainbow, Abraham's Ram, Isaac's Wells, Jacob's Ladder, Issachar's Burdens, Jacob's Scepter, Balaam's Shiloh, Moses' Rod, Joshua's Sun and Moon that stood still, Elijah's Mantle, Elisha's Staff, Gideon's Fleece, Samuel's Horn of Oil, David's Slingshot, Isaiah's Fig Poultice, Hezekiah's Sundial, Daniel's Visions, Amos' Burden, and Malachi's Sun of Righteousness.

It's All About Jesus

He is Peter's Shadow, Stephen's Signs and Wonders, Paul's Handkerchiefs and Aprons, and John's Pearly White City.

He is Father to the Orphan, Husband to the Widow, to the traveler in the night He is the Bright and Morning Star, to those who walk in the Lonesome Valley He is the Lily of the Valley, the Rose of Sharon, and Honey in the Rock.

He is the Brightness of God's Glory, the Express Image of His Person, the King of Glory, the Pearl of Great Price, the Rock in a Weary Land, the Cup that runneth over, the Rod and Staff that comfort, and the Government of our life is upon His shoulders.

He is Jesus of Nazareth, the Son of the living God! My Savior, my Companion, my Lord and King!

Author Unknown

The Blood of Jesus 'A' to 'Z'

Atones for the soul	Leviticus 27:11
Brings us into the covenant of grace	Matthew 26:28
Cleanses us from all sin	I John 1:7
Delivers God's people from judgment	Exodus 12:13
Everlasting in its value	Hebrews 13:20
Furnishes the only ground of peace with God	Colossians 1:20
Gives us access into His presence	Hebrews 10:19-21
Has already obtained for us redemption	Ephesians 1:7
Imparts eternal life	John 6:54
Justifies us in the sight of God	Romans 5:9
Keeps us in the holy of holies	Hebrews 9:22-26
Links us to God's electing purpose	I Peter 1:2
Makes us nigh to Him	Ephesians 2:13
Never needs to be offered again	Hebrews 9:12
Overcomes the power of Satan	Revelation 12:11
Purchases us	Acts 20:28
Quenches the righteous wrath of God	Romans 3:25
Redeems us from our state of ruin	I Peter 1:18-19
Speaks to God and to us of salvation	Hebrews 12:24
Tunes the voices of the saints in holy song	Revelation 5:9
Unites us in Christian communion	I Corinthians 10:16
Victorious over Tribulation	Revelation 7:14
Washes from us every stain	Revelation 1:6
X-ian's hope, is the	I Timothy 1:1
Yields the price that bought the church	Acts 20:28
Zealous of good words, makes us	Titus 2:14

Key Points in the Life of Jesus

The birth of Jesus	Luke 1-2
The baptism of Jesus	Mark 1:9-11
The temptation of Jesus	Luke 4:1-13
The sending out of the twelve disciples by Jesus	Matthew 10
The clearing of the temple by Jesus	John 2:12-25
The Sermon on the Mount by Jesus	Matthew 5:1-7:29
The walking on the water by Jesus	John 6:16-21
The Kingdom parables of Jesus	Matthew 13:1-52
The feeding of the 5,000 by Jesus	Mark 6:30-44
The meeting between Nicodemus and Jesus	John 3:1-21
The transfiguration of Jesus	Matthew 17:1-13
The raising of Lazarus by Jesus	John 11:1-46
The signs of the end times as told by Jesus	Matthew 24
The triumphal entry into Jerusalem by Jesus	Mark 11:1-11
The widow's offering and Jesus	Mark 12:41-44
The Last Supper and the comments of Jesus	Luke 22:7-38
The washing of the disciple's feet by Jesus	John 13:1-17
The Garden of Gethsemane and prayer of Jesus	Matthew 26:36-56
The betrayal by Judas Iscariot of Jesus	Luke 22:1-53
The denial by Peter of Jesus	Luke 22:54-62
The crucifixion of Jesus	Matthew 26:57-27:66
The resurrection and ascension of Jesus	Luke 24

The Prayers of Jesus

His prayer before temptation	Luke 3:21; 4:1-13
His prayer before the selection of the disciples	Luke 6:12-16
His prayer before the Sermon on the Mount	Luke 6:12, 17-49
His common practice of prayer	Luke 4:16-32; Mark 1:21-22
His teaching about the manner of prayer	Matthew 6:5-8
His teaching as to the matter of prayer	Matthew 6:9-15
His teaching as to earnestness in prayer	Matthew 7:7-11; Luke 11:5-10; 18:1-8
His teaching as to the objective of prayer	Luke 11:11-13
His prayer after serving the people	Matthew 14:22-23
His prayer before his glory was manifested	Luke 9:28-36
His story about vain prayer	Luke 18:9-14
His prayer in joy	Luke 10:17-24; Matthew 11:25-30
His teaching as to the power of prayer	Matthew 18:19-20; Mark 11:22-25
His warning about too much formal prayer	Luke 20:45-47; Matthew 6:7-8
His exhortation to vigilant prayer	Luke 12:34-36; Matthew 24:32; 25:13
His promises to those who pray	John 14:12-17; 15:7-10; 16:23-24
His prayer for all believers	John 17
His prayer for Himself	Matthew 26:36-44
His prayers from the cross	Luke 23:34, 46

The Miracles of Jesus

Healing Miracles	**Matthew**	**Mark**	**Luke**	**John**
Man with leprosy	8:2-4	1:40-44	5:12-4	
Roman centurion's servant	8:5-13		7:1-10	
Peter's mother-in-law	8:14-15	1:30-31	4:38-39	
Two men from Gadara	8:28-34	5:1-15	8:26-39	
Paralyzed man	9:2-7	2:3-12	5:18-26	
Woman with bleeding	9:20-22	5:25-34	8:43-48	
Two blind men	9:27-31			
Mute, demon-possessed man	9:32-33			
Man with a shriveled hand	12:10-13	3:1-5	6:6-10	
Blind, mute, demon-possessed	12:22		11:14	
Canaanite woman's daughter	15:21-28	7:24-30		
Boy with a demon	17:14-21	9:17-29	9:38-43	
Two blind men (Bartimaeus)	20:29-34	10:46-52	18:35-43	
Deaf mute		7:31-37		
Possessed man in synagogue		1:23-26	4:33-35	
Blind man at Bethsaida		8:22-26		
Crippled woman			13:10-17	
Man with dropsy			14:1-4	
Ten men with leprosy			17:11-19	
The high priest's servant			22:50-51	
Official's son at Capernaum				4:46-54
Sick man at pool of Bethesda				5:1-15
Man born blind				9:1-41
Miracles demonstrating the power over nature				
Calming the storm	8:23-27	4:37-41	8:22-25	
Walking on water	14:22-33	6:47-52		6:16-21
Feeding the 5,000	14:13-21	6:30-44	9:10-17	6:1-13
Feeding the 4,000	15:32-38	8:1-10		
Coin in fish	17:24-27			
Fig tree withered	21:18-22	11:12-14, 20-25		
Large catch of fish			5:4-11	
Water turned to wine				2:1-11
Second large catch of fish				21:1-11
Miracles of raising the dead				
Jairus's daughter	9:18-26	5:21-43	8:40-56	
Widow's son at Nain			7:11-17	
Lazarus				11:1-44

The Teaching of Jesus on Various Topics

The Beatitudes	Matthew 5:1-12
Being Born Again	John 3:1-21
Blasphemy Against the Spirit	Matthew 12:31-32
The Bread of Life	John 6:25-59
The Brother who Sins	Matthew 18:15-20
The Cost of Following Jesus	Luke 9:57-62
Discipleship	Luke 14:25-35
Divorce	Matthew 19:1-12
Fig Tree	Mark 13:28-31
Friend in Need	John 11:5-8
The Gift of Living Water	John 4:1-26
Giving to Caesar	Mark 12:13-17
The Golden Rule	Luke 6:31
The Good Samaritan	Luke 10:25-37
The Good Shepherd	John 10:1-21
The Great Banquet	Luke 14:15-24
The Greatest Commandment	Matthew 22:34-40
The Greatest in the Kingdom	Matthew 18:1-9

It's All About Jesus

The Lamp on a Stand	Luke 8:16-18
The Lord's Prayer	Matthew 6:5-15
The Lost Coin	John 15:8-10
The Lost Sheep	Matthew 18:12-14
Moneylender	Luke 7:41-43
Murder and Adultery	Matthew 5
The Narrow Door	Luke 13:22-30
The Net	Matthew 13:47-50
The Parable of the Mustard Seed	Mark 4:26-29
The Parable of the Sower	Matthew 13
The Parable of the Talents	Matthew 25:14-30
The Parable of the Ten Virgins	Matthew 25:1-13
The Parable of the Vineyard	Matthew 20:1-16
The Parable of the Wedding	Matthew 22:1-14
The Persistent Widow	Matthew 18:2-8
The Pharisee and the Tax Collector	John 18:10-14
Prayer	Luke 11:1-13
The Prodigal Son	John 15:11-32
A Prophet Without Honor	Mark 6:1-6
Rest for the Weary	Matthew 11:25-30
The Rich Man and Lazarus	John 16:19-31

It's All About Jesus

The Rich Young Ruler	Matthew 19:16-30
Sending Out of the Twelve	Matthew 10
The Sermon on the Mount	Matthew 5-7
The Sheep and the Goats	Matthew 25:31-46
The Sign of Jonah	Matthew 12:38-45
The Six Woes	Luke 11:37-54
Sorrow Over Jerusalem	Luke 13:31-34
The Two Sons	Matthew 21:28-32
The Unmerciful Servant	Matthew 18:21-35
Valuable Pearl	Matthew 13:45-46
The Vine and Branches	John 15:1-17
Watchful Servants	John 12:35-40
Watchfulness	Luke 12:35-48
The Way, the Truth, and the Life	John 14:5-14
Wealth	Matthew 19:16-30
Who Will Be the Greatest?	Luke 9:46-50
Wise and Foolish Builders	Luke 6:43-49

The Resurrection Appearances of Jesus

Appearance	Location	Time Period	
The empty tomb	Jerusalem	Sunday	Luke 24:1-12
To Mary Magdalene	Jerusalem	Sunday	John 20:11-18
To other women	Jerusalem	Sunday	Matthew 28:9-10
Two on road to Emmaus	On road	Sunday	Luke 24:13-32
To Peter	Jerusalem	Sunday	John 15:5
To ten disciples	Jerusalem	Sunday	Luke 24:36-43
To eleven disciples	Jerusalem	Sunday	John 20:26-31
To seven disciples	Sea of Galilee	Some time Later	John 21:1-23
To eleven disciples	Galilee	Some time Later	Matthew 28:16-20
To more than 500 people	Unknown	Some time Later	I Corinthians 15:6
To James	Unknown	Some time Later	I Corinthians 15:7
To the disciples	Mount of Olives	40 days Later	Luke 24:36-51
To Paul the Apostle	Damascus	Several years Later	Acts 9:1-19

Divine Footsteps

Christ has come, the Light of the world. Long ages may yet elapse before his beams have reduced the world to order and beauty, and clothed a purified humanity with light as with a garment. But he has come: the Revealer of the snares and chasms that lurk in darkness, the Rebuker of every evil thing that prowls by night, the Stiller of the storm-winds of passion, the Quickener of all that is wholesome, the Adorner of all that is beautiful, the Reconciler of contradictions, the Harmonizer of discords, the Healer of diseases, the Savior from sin.

He has come: the Torch of truth, the Anchor of hope, the Pillar of faith, the Rock for strength, the Refuge for security, the Fountain for refreshment, the Vine for gladness, the Rose for beauty, the Lamb for tenderness, the Friend for counsel, the Brother for love. Jesus Christ has trod the world. The trace of the divine footsteps will never be obliterated.

Peter Bayne
from "The Testimony of Christ to Christianity," 1862

Joseph as a Type of Jesus

Similar Circumstances	Joseph	Jesus
1. Both were shepherds	Genesis 37:2	John 10:11, 27-29
2. Both loved by their fathers	Genesis 37:3	Matthew 3:17
3. Both had trouble with brothers	Genesis 37:4	John 7:4-5
4. Both sent by their fathers	Genesis 37:13-14	Hebrews 2:11
5. Both plotted against by others	Genesis 37:20	John 11:53
6. Both had robes taken from them	Genesis 37:23	John 19:23-24
7. Both taken to Egypt	Genesis 37:26	Matthew 2:14-15
8. Both sold for the price of a slave	Genesis 37:28	Matthew 26:15
9. Both tempted	Genesis 39:37	Matthew 4:1
10. Both falsely accused	Genesis 39:16-18	Matthew 26:59-60
11. Both bound in chains	Genesis 39:20	Matthew 27:2
12. Both placed with two prisoners	Genesis 40:2-3	Luke 23:32
13. Both exalted after their suffering	Genesis 41:40	Philippians 2:9-11
14. Both 30 years old when recognized	Genesis 41:40	Luke 3:23
15. Both of them wept	Genesis 42:44	John 19:35
16. Both forgave wrongdoers	Genesis 45:1-15	Luke 23:34
17. Both saved their nation	Genesis 45:7	Matthew 1:21
18. Both had hurt turned to good	Genesis 50:20	I Corinthians 2:7-8

Titles for Jesus

Advocate
If anyone sins, we have an Advocate with the Father, Jesus Christ the righteous (I John 2:1)

All in All
Christ is All and in all (Colossians 3:11)

Almighty
I am . . . the Almighty (Revelation 1:8)

Alpha and Omega
I am the Alpha and the Omega (Revelation 22:13)

Amen
These are the words of the Amen (Revelation 3:14)

Ancient of Days
Thrones were set in place, and the Ancient of Days took His seat (Daniel 7:9)

Anointed One (Messiah)
Know and understand this: From the issuing of the decree to restore and rebuild Jerusalem until the Anointed One, the Ruler comes, there will be seven "sevens," and sixty-two "sevens" (Daniel 9:25)

Apostle of Our Profession
Consider the Apostle . . . of our profession, Christ Jesus (Hebrews 3:1)

Arm of the Lord
To whom has the Arm of the Lord been revealed? (Isaiah 53:1)

It's All About Jesus

Atoning Sacrifice

He is the Atoning Sacrifice for our sins, and not only for ours but also for the sins of the whole world (I John 2:2)

Baby

You will find a Baby wrapped in clothes and lying in a manger (Luke 2:12)

Banner for the Peoples

In that day the Root of Jesse will stand as a Banner for the Peoples (Isaiah 11:10)

Beloved

He has made us accepted in the Beloved (Ephesians 1:6)

Blessed and Only Potentate

He who is the Blessed and only Potentate, the King of kings and Lord of lords (I Timothy 6:15)

Boy Jesus

The Boy Jesus stayed behind in Jerusalem (Luke 2:43)

Branch

A shoot will come up from the stump of Jesse; from his roots a branch will bear fruit (Isaiah 11:1)

Bread of Life

I am the Bread of Life (John 6:35)

Bridegroom

The time will come when the Bridegroom shall be taken from them (Matthew 9:15)

Bright and Morning Star

I am the Bright and Morning Star (Revelation 22:16)

It's All About Jesus

Brother
Isn't this Mary's Son and the Brother of James, Joses, Judas, and Simon? Aren't His sisters here with us? (Mark 6:35)

Carpenter
Isn't this the Carpenter? (Mark 6:3)

Chief Cornerstone
With Christ Jesus Himself as the Chief Cornerstone (Ephesians 2:20)

Christ
We have found the Messiah, (that is, the Christ) (John 1:41)

Dayspring
The Dayspring from on high has visited us (Luke 1:78)

Desire of All Nations
And they shall come to the Desire of all nations (Haggai 2:7)

Door
I am the Door (John 10:9)

Everlasting Father
And He will be called . . . Everlasting Father (Isaiah 9:6)

Exact Representation of His Being
The Son is the . . . Exact Representation of His being (Hebrews 1:3)

Faithful and True Witness
These are the words of the . . . Faithful and True Witness (Revelation 3:14)

It's All About Jesus

First and Last
I am the First and Last (Revelation 1:17)

Firstborn over All Creation
He is . . . the Firstborn over all Creation (Colossians 1:15)

Friend
And they say, "here is . . . a Friend" (Matthew 11:19)

Galilean
Pilate asked if the man was a Galilean (Luke 23:6)

God
Thomas said to Him, "My Lord and my God!" (John 20:28)

Good Shepherd
I am the Good Shepherd (John 10:11)

Guarantee of a Better Covenant
Jesus has become the Guarantee of a better covenant (Hebrews 7:22)

Head
Speaking the truth in love, we will in all things grow up into Him who is the Head, that is, Christ (Ephesians 4:15)

Head of the Church
Christ is the Head of the Church (Ephesians 5:23)

Heir of All things
But in these last days He has spoken to us by His Son, whom He appointed Heir of all things, and through whom He made the universe (Hebrews 1:2)

High Priest
He has become a High Priest forever, in the order of Melchizedek (Hebrews 6:20)

Holy One
I know who you are—the Holy One of God! (Mark 1:24)

Horn of Salvation
He has raised up a Horn of Salvation for us (Luke 1:69)

I Am
"I tell you the truth," Jesus answered . . . "I Am!" (John 8:58)

Image of the Invisible God
He is the Image of the Invisible God (Colossians 1:15)

Immanuel
"The virgin will be with child and will give birth to a Son, and they will call Him Immanuel"—which means, "God with us" (Matthew 1:23)

Indescribable Gift
Thanks be to God for His Indescribable Gift (II Corinthians 9:15)

Jesus
You are to give Him the name Jesus, because He will save His people from their sins (Matthew 1:21)

Jesus Christ
Peter, an apostle of Jesus Christ (I Peter 1:1)

Jew
The Samaritan woman said to Him, "You are a Jew" (John 4:9)

It's All About Jesus

Judge
He is the one whom God appointed as Judge of the living and the dead (Acts 10:42)

King
Rejoice greatly, O daughter of Zion! Shout, Daughter of Jerusalem! See, your King comes to you, righteous and having salvation, gentle and riding on a donkey, on a colt, the foal of a donkey (Zechariah 9:9)

King of Kings
God, the blessed and only Ruler, the King of kings and Lord of lords (I Timothy 6:15)

Lamb of God
Look, the Lamb of God, who takes away the sin of the world! (John 1:29)

Last Adam
The first man Adam became a living being; the last Adam, a life-giving Spirit (I Corinthians 15:45)

Leader and Commander
See, I have made Him a . . . Leader and Commander of the peoples (Isaiah 55:4)

Life
I am . . . the Life (John 14:6)

Light of the World
I am the Light of the World (John 8:14)

Lily of the Valley
I am the . . . Lily of the Valley (Song of Solomon 2:1)

It's All About Jesus

Lion of the Tribe of Judah
Do not weep! See, the Lion of the Tribe of Judah . . . has triumphed (Revelation 5:5)

Living One
I am the Living One (Revelation 1:18)

Living Water
If you knew the gift of God . . . you would have asked Him and He would have given you Living Water (John 4:10)

Lord
And every tongue confess that Jesus Christ is Lord, to the glory of God the Father (Philippians 2:11)

Lord Our Righteousness
This is the name by which He will be called: The Lord Our Righteousness (Jeremiah 23:6)

Man
The Man Christ Jesus, who gave Himself as a ransom for all men (I Timothy 2:5-6)

Man of Sorrows
He was despised and rejected by men, a Man of Sorrows and familiar with suffering (Isaiah 53:3)

Mediator
For there is one God and one Mediator between God and men, the man Christ Jesus (I Timothy 2:5)

Messenger of the Covenant
"See . . . the Lord you are seeking will come to His temple; the Messenger of the Covenant, whom you desire, will come," says the Lord Almighty (Malachi 3:1)

It's All About Jesus

Mighty God
And He will be called . . . Mighty God (Isaiah 9:6)

Nazarene
*And He went and lived in a town called Nazareth. So was fulfilled what was said through the prophets: "He will be called a Nazarene" (*Matthew 2:23)

Offspring of the Woman
And I will put enmity . . . between your Offspring and hers; He will crush your head, and you will strike His heel (Genesis 3:15)

Only Begotten Son
For God so loved the world that He gave His Only Begotten Son (John 3:16)

Our Hope
Christ Jesus Our Hope (I Timothy 1:1)

Our Passover
Christ, Our Passover Lamb, has been sacrificed
(I Corinthians 5:7—Exodus 12:1-27)

Overseer
For you were like sheep going astray, but now you have returned to the Shepherd and Overseer of your souls (I Peter 2:25)

Physician
Jesus said to them, "Surely you will quote this proverb to Me: 'Physician, heal yourself!'" (Luke 4:23)

Pioneer of Our Faith
Looking to Jesus the Pioneer . . . of Our Faith (Hebrews 12:2)

Pioneer of Our Salvation
But it was fitting that He, for whom and by whom all things exist . . . should make the Pioneer of Their Salvation perfect through suffering (Hebrews 1:10)

Prince of Peace
And He will be called . . . Prince of Peace (Isaiah 9:6)

Prophet
The crowds answered, "This is Jesus, the Prophet from Nazareth in Galilee" (Matthew 21:11)

Rabboni
She turned toward Him and cried out . . . "Rabboni" (John 20:16)

Radiance of God's Glory
The Son is the Radiance of God's glory (Hebrews 1:3)

Ransom
Christ Jesus, who gave Himself as a Ransom for all men (I Timothy 2:5-6)

Redeemer
I know that my Redeemer lives, and that in the end He will stand upon the earth (Job 19:25)

Resurrection and the Life
I am the Resurrection and the Life. He who believes in Me will live, even though he dies (John 11:25)

Rock
They drank from the spiritual Rock that accompanied them, and that Rock was Christ (I Corinthians 10:4)

Root and the Offspring of David
I am the Root and the Offspring of David (Revelation 22:16)

Rose of Sharon
I am the Rose of Sharon (Song of Songs 2:1)

Ruler of God's Creation
The Ruler of God's Creation (Revelation 3:14)

Savior
This is indeed the Christ, Savior of the world (John 4:42)

Scepter
A Scepter will rise out of Israel (Numbers 24:17)

Servant
Here is My Servant whom I have chosen (Matthew 12:18)

Shiloh
The scepter shall not depart from Judah, nor a lawgiver from between his feet, until Shiloh comes; and to Him shall be the obedience of the people (Genesis 49:10)

Son of David
A record of the genealogy of Jesus Christ the Son of David (Matthew 1:1)

Son of Man
Just as the Son of Man did not come to be served, but to serve, and to give His life as a ransom for many (Matthew 20:28)

Star
A Star will come out of Jacob (Numbers 24:17)

It's All About Jesus

Sun of Righteousness
But unto you who revere and worshipfully fear My name shall the Sun of Righteousness arise with healing in His wings and His beams, and you shall go forth and gambol like calves released from the stall and leap for joy (Malachi 4:2)

Teacher
We know You are a Teacher who has come from God (John 3:2)

The True Vine
I am the True Vine (John 15:1)

The Truth
I am . . . the Truth (John 14:6)

The Way
I am the Way (John 14:6)

Wonderful Counselor
And He will be called Wonderful Counselor (Isaiah 9:6)

Word
His name is the Word of God (Revelation 19:13)

In the beginning was the Word, and the Word was with God, and the Word was God. He was with God in the beginning (John 1:1-2)

The Word became flesh and lived for a while among us (John 1:14)

> *You search the Scriptures because you believe they give you eternal life. But the Scriptures point to me!*
>
> John 5:39-40

Bible Study Helps

ABUSIVE BEHAVIOR
Romans 12:10
Romans 12:18-19
I Corinthians 10:31
I Thessalonians 5:15
James 1:20

ACCOUNTABILITY
Joshua 7:1-15
Judges 6:1-16
Ecclesiastes 12:13-14
Romans 14:1-22

ADULTERY
Isaiah 1:1-31
Hosea 1:1-11
Matthew 5:27-32
Luke 16:16-18
John 8:1-11

ADVICE
Proverbs 1:1-9
Proverbs 6:20-24
Proverbs 10:1-21
Mark 10:17-31

AFFECTIONS
Proverbs 4:23-27

ALCOHOLISM
Proverbs 20:1
Proverbs 23:29-35
I Corinthians 15:33
II Peter 2:19

ANGER
Matthew 5:21-26
Ephesians 4:26-32
James 3:6

ANXIETY
Psalm 16:11
Psalm 37:1,7
Proverbs 16:7
Isaiah 41:10

ARGUMENTS
Proverbs 15:1-9
Proverbs 26:17-28
Philippians 2:12-18
Titus 3:1:11

ATTITUDE
Philippians 2:5-11
Philippians 4:4-9

BELIEF
Romans 10:5-13
James 2:14-24

BEREAVEMENT
Deuteronomy 31:8
Psalm 23:1-6
Psalm 27:10
Psalm 119:50

BITTERNESS
Hebrews 12:14-17
I John 3:11-24

CHOICES
Proverbs 1:1-19
Proverbs 13:1-16
Matthew 9:9-13

COMFORT
Job 16:1-22
Lamentations 3:21-26
II Corinthians 1:3-11

COMPLAINING
Philippians 2:12-18

CONFIDENCE
Matthew 10:26-42
Acts 5:17-26

CONFLICTS
James 4:1-12

CONSCIENCE
Proverbs 28:13-18
Acts 23:1
Acts 24:16
I Timothy 3:8-9
Hebrews 10:21-22
I Peter 3:16

CRITICISM
Matthew 7:1-5
Luke 17:1-10
Galatians 5:13-26

DECEIT
Exodus 20:1-21

DEPRESSION
I Kings 19:1-9
Psalm 42:1-11

DESIRES
Psalm 97:1-12

DESPAIR
Exodus 14:1-14
Psalm 40:1-17

DIFFICULTIES
Romans 8:28
II Corinthians 4:17
Hebrews 12:7-11
Revelation 3:19

DISAPPOINTMENT
Psalm 43:5
Psalm 55:22
Psalm 126:6
John 14:27
II Corinthians 4:8-10

DISCOURAGEMENT
Joshua 1:9
Psalm 27:14
Colossians 1:5
I Peter 1:3-9
I John 5:14

DISCERNMENT
Matthew 7:1-12
James 1:2-8

DISHONESTY
Proverbs 20:23-30

DISOBEDIENCE
Genesis 3:1-24
I Chronicles 13:1-14

DIVORCE & REMARRIAGE
Malachi 2:15-16
Matthew 19:8-9
I Corinthians 7:10-15

DRINKING
Proverbs 23:29-35
Ephesians 5:15-20

ENCOURAGEMENT
I Thessalonians 5:1-28
I Peter 1:1-13

ENTHUSIASM
Colossians 3:18-25

ENVY
Deuteronomy 5:21
I Kings 21:1-29

ETERNAL LIFE
Luke 18:18-30
John 3:1-21
John 6:60-71
John 17:1-26
I John 5:1-13

FAULTS
Matthew 7:1-5
Ephesians 4:1-16

FEAR
Joshua 1:1-18
Psalm 27:1
Psalm 56:11
Psalm 91`:1-6
Psalm 121:1-8
Proverbs 29:25

FEELINGS
Romans 5:9-21

FOOLISHNESS
Psalm 14:1-7
Proverbs 9:1-18
I Corinthians 2:6-16

FORGIVENESS
Psalm 51:1-19
Matthew 6:5-15
Matthew 18:21-35
Romans 12:1-21
I John 1:1-10

FRIENDSHIP
Proverbs 17:1-28
John 15:1-17

FRUSTRATION
Ephesians 6:1-4

GAMBLING
Proverbs 15:16
Proverbs 23:4-5
Luke 12:15
I Timothy 6:9

GENTLENESS
II Timothy 2:14-26
James 3:1-18

GOSSIP
Exodus 23:1-9
Proverbs 25:18-28
II Thessalonians 3:6-15

GREED
James 4:1-17

GUILT
Psalm 32:1-2
Romans 8:1-17
Colossians 2:9-17
I John 3:11-24

HABITS
I John 3:1-24

HAPPINESS
Matthew 5:1-12
I Timothy 6:3-10

HEAVEN
John 14:1-14
Colossians 3:1-17

HELL
Matthew 25:41-46
Romans 1:18-32
Revelation 210:1-15

HELP
Psalm 46:1-11
Galatians 6:1-10

HOPE
Romans 5:1-11
I Thessalonians 4:13-18

HURT
Psalm 55:22
Psalm 56:3-4
Psalm 121:1-8
I Peter 5:7

IMMORALITY
I Corinthians 6:1-20
Revelation 9:13-21

INDECISIVENESS
John 3:22-36

INFERIORITY
Psalm 63:3
Psalm 86:13
Psalm 139:13-16

I Corinthians 1:26-29
I Peter 2:9-10

INTEGRITY
Psalm 25:1-22
Luke 16:1-15

JEALOUSY
Romans 13:1-14

KINDNESS
Luke 6:27-36
Colossians 3:1-17

LAZINESS
II Thessalonians 3:6-15
II Peter 3:1-18

LONELINESS
Psalm 23:1-6
Isaiah 41:10
Matthew 28:20
Hebrews 13:5-6

LUST
Mark 7:20-23
Romans 6:12
I Thessalonians 4:3-8
James 1:14-15

LYING
Proverbs 17:20
Proverbs 19:9
Proverbs 24:24
Proverbs 29:12
Proverbs 25:28
Matthew 5:37
Ephesians 4:17-32

MATERIALISM
Matthew 6:19-24

MORALITY
Romans 2:1-16
Romans 12:1-8

MOTIVES
Jeremiah 17:1-18
James 4:1-12

OBEDIENCE
Deuteronomy 30:11-19
James 5:1-6

PAIN
Hebrews 12:1-13

PEACE
Psalm 3:1-8
John 14:31
Romans 5:1-11

PRIORITIES
Proverbs 3:1-35
Matthew 6:25-34

PROBLEMS
James 1:1-18

PROCRASTINATION
Proverbs 10:1-32
Proverbs 26:1-28

QUARRELS
Proverbs 13:1-10
Titus 3:1-11
James 4:1-12

RELATIONSHIPS
II Corinthians 6:14-18
Ephesians 2:11-22

RESENTMENT
James 1:1-27

REVENGE
Romans 12:17-21

SELF-CENTEREDNESS
Mark 8:31-38
I Peter 1:14-25

SELFISHNESS
Mark 8:31-38
James 4:1-10

SEX
Proverbs 5:15-21
I Corinthians 7:1-11
I Thessalonians 4:1-8

SICKNESS
Psalm 41:3
Psalm 103:3
Matthew 43:23
John 11:4
James 5:13-15

SIN
Isaiah 53:5-6
Isaiah 59:1-2
John 8:34
Romans 3:23
Romans 6:23
Galatians 6:7-8

STRESS
Romans 5:1-5
Philippians 4:4-9

SUFFERING
Romans 8:18
II Corinthians 1:5
Philippians 3:10
II Timothy 2:12
James 1:2-8
I Peter 1:6-7

SUICIDE
Job 14:5
Romans 14:7
I Corinthians 6:19-20
James 4:7

TEMPTATION
Psalm 94:17-18
Proverbs 28:13
I Corinthians 10:12-13
Hebrews 4:14-16
James 1:2-14

TERMINAL ILLNESS
Jeremiah 29:11
II Corinthians 12:9
I Thessalonians 5:18
II Timothy 2:112

THANKFULNESS
Psalm 92:1-15
Romans 1:18-23
Ephesians 2:1-10

WAITING
Psalm 27:1-14
Psalm 40:14
Matthew 24:32-51

WEAKNESS
II Corinthians 12:1-10
I John 3:1-11

WILL OF GOD
Psalm 37:4
Psalm 91:1-2
Proverbs 3:5-6
Proverbs 4:26
Romans 14:5
Galatians 6:4
Ephesians 5:15-21
Philippians 2:12-13
I Thessalonians 4:3
I Peter 3:17

WISDOM
Psalm 119:97-112
Proverbs 1:1-7
Ecclesiastes 8:1-8
Luke 2:23-40
James 1:2-8

WORRY
Psalm 37:1-11
Matthew 6:25-34
Philippians 4:4-9

Part V
Books Will Help You Grow in Character

Charles "Tremendous" Jones' Favorite Quotations about Books

Oswald Chambers' great love for books is revealed in a letter to his sister.

> *My box has at last arrived. My books! I cannot tell you what they are to me—silent, wealthy, loyal lovers. To look at them, to handle them, and to reread them! I do thank God for my books with every fiber of my being. Friends that are ever true and ever your own. Why, I could have almost cried for excess joy when I got hold of them again. I see them all just at my elbow now—Plato, Wordsworth, Myers, Bradley, Halyburton, St. Augustine, Browning, Tennyson, Amiel, etc. I know them, I wish you could see how they look at me, a quiet calm look of certain acquaintance.*

Oswald Chambers

* * *

Except a living man, there is nothing more wonderful than a book!—a message to us from the dead—from human souls whom we never saw, who lived, perhaps, thousands of miles away; and yet these, in those little sheets of paper, speak to us, amuse us, terrify us, teach us, comfort us, open their hearts to us as brothers . . . I say we ought to reverence books, to look at them as useful and mighty things. If they are good and true, whether they are about religion or politics, farming, trade, or medicine, they are the message of Christ, the maker of all things, the teacher of all truth.

Charles Kingsley

A book is the only place in which you can examine a fragile thought without breaking it, or explore an explosive idea without fear it will go off in your face . . . It is one of the few havens remaining where a man's mind can get both provocation and privacy.

Edward P. Morgan

* * *

A house without books is like a room without windows. No man has a right to bring up his children without surrounding them with books, if he has the means to buy them. It is a wrong to his family. Children learn to read by being in the presence of books. The love of knowledge comes with reading and grows upon it. And the love of knowledge, in a young mind, is almost a warrant against the inferior excitement of passions and vices.

Horace Mann

* * *

Just the knowledge that a good book is awaiting one at the end of a long day makes that day happier.

Kathleen Norris

* * *

The books which help you most are those which make you think the most.

Theodore Parker

* * *

Everything comes to him who waits. Except a loaned book.

Kin Hubbard

How many a man had dated a new era in his life from the reading of a book.

Henry David Thoreau

* * *

When I get a little money, I buy books; and if any is left, I buy food and clothes.

Desiderius Erasmus

* * *

There is more treasure in books than in all the pirates' loot on Treasure Island … And best of all, you can enjoy these riches every day of your life.

Walt Disney

* * *

Read the best books first, or you may not have a chance to read them at all.

Henry David Thoreau

* * *

If we encountered a man of rare intellect, we should ask him what books he read.

Ralph Waldo Emerson

* * *

I cannot live without books.

Thomas Jefferson

* * *

Books are the bees which carry the quickening pollen from one to another mind.

James Russell Lowell

* * *

A drop of ink may make a million think.

Lord Byron

* * *

Books are the quietest and most constant of friends; they are the most accessible and wisest of counselors, and the most patient of teachers.

Charles W. Eliot

* * *

The first time I read an excellent book, it is to me just as if I had gained a new friend. When I read over a book I have perused before, it resembles the meeting with an old one.

Oliver Goldsmith

* * *

A room without books is like a body without a soul.

Cicero

Recommended Books for Growth in Character

Ken Blanchard and Phil Hodges, *Lead Like Jesus: Lessons from the Greatest Leadership Role Model of All Time* (Nashville, TN: Thomas Nelson, 2008).

Ken Blanchard, Bill Hybels, and Phil Hodges, *Leadership by the Book: Tools to Transform Your Workplace* (New York: William Morrow, 1999).

Ken Blanchard and Phil Hodges, *The Most Loving Place in Town: A Modern Day Parable for the Church* (Nashville, TN: Thomas Nelson, 2008).

John Bunyan, *The Pilgrim's Progress* (Peabody, MA: Hendrickson Publishers, 2004).

L.B. Cowman (Mrs. Charles Cowman), *Streams in the Desert* (Nashville, TN: Zondervan, 1999).

Gregory Dixon, *Acres of Diamonds*: *The Russell Conwell Story* (Mechanicsburg, PA: Executive Books, 2005).

François Fénelon, *The Seeking Heart* (Jacksonville, FL: Seed Sowers, 1992).

Richard J. Foster, *Celebration of Discipline: The Path to Spiritual Growth* (San Francisco: HarperCollins, 1988).

George Grant, *Carry A Big Stick: The Uncommon Heroism of Theodore Roosevelt* (Nashville, TN: Cumberland House, 1996).

Jeanne Guyon, *Jeanne Guyon: An Autobiography* (New Kensington, PA: Whitaker House, 1997).

Jack Hartman, *Trust God for Your Finances* (Dunedin, FL: Lamplight Publications, 1993).

James C. Hunter, *The Servant: A Simple Story about the True Essence of Leadership* (London: Crown Business, 1998).

Charlie "Tremendous" Jones, *Forgiveness is Tremendous* (Mechanicsburg, PA: Executive Books, 2007).

Charlie "Tremendous" Jones, *Life is Tremendous* (Mechanicsburg, PA: Executive Books, 1968).

Lori Beth Jones, The *Four Elements of Success: A Simple Personality Profile That Will Transform Your Team* (Nashville, TN: Thomas Nelson, 2006).

Tim LaHaye and Bob Phillips, *Anger Is a Choice* (Grand Rapids, MI: Zondervan, 1982).

R.G. LeTourneau, *Mover of Men and Mountains* (Chicago, IL: Moody Publishers, 1967).

James Mansfield, *Then Darkness Fled: The Liberating Wisdom of Booker T. Washington* (Nashville, TN: Cumberland House, 2002).

Stephen Mansfield, *Never Give In: The Extraordinary Character of Winston Churchill* (Nashville, TN: Cumberland House, 1996).

David McCasland, *Oswald Chambers: Abandoned to God* (Grand Rapids, MI: Zondervan, 1993).

Henrietta C. Mears, *What The Bible is All About* (Ventura, CA: Regal Books, 2002).

Catherine Millard and Maxwell Edgar, *Great American Statesmen and Heroes:* (Traverse City, MI: Horizon Books, 1995).

George Mūller, *The Autobiography of George Müller* (New Kensington, PA: Whitaker House, 1984).

Watchman Nee, *The Normal Christian Life* (Fort Washington, PA: Christian Literature Crusade, 1971).

William J. Peterson, *The Complete Book of Hymns* (Carol Stream, IL: Tyndale House, 2006).

Bob Phillips and Kimberly Alyn, *How to Deal with Annoying People* (Eugene, OR: Harvest House, 2005).

Bob Phillips, *Overcoming Anxiety and Depression: Practical Tools to Help You Deal with Negative Emotions* (Eugene, OR: Harvest House, 2007).

Donald Phillips, *Founding Fathers on Leadership: Classic Teamwork in Changing Times* (New York: Grand Central Publishing, 1998).

Ron Price, *Finding Hidden Treasures* (Mechanicsburg, PA: Executive Books, 2005).

Dan Reiland, *From a Father's Heart* (Nashville, TN: Thomas Nelson, 1999).

Michael Richardson, *Amazing Faith: The Authorized Biography of Bill Bright, Founder of Campus Crusade for Christ* (Colorado Springs, CO: WaterBrook Press, 2000).

Earl O. Roe, Editor, *Dream Big: The Henrietta Mears Story* (Ventura, CA: Regal Books, 1991).

Oswald Sanders, *Spiritual Leadership* (Chicago, IL: Moody Press, 1980).

Betty Skinner, *Daws: A Man Who Trusted God* (Colorado Springs, CO: NavPress, 1974)
Charles H. Spurgeon, *All of Grace* (London: Passmore and Alabaster, 1886).

A.W. Tozer, *The Best of A. W. Tozer One* (Camp Hill, PA: Wingspread Publications, 2007).

David J. Vaughan, *Give Me Liberty: The Uncompromising Statesmanship of Patrick Henry* (Nashville, TN: Cumberland House, 1997).

David J. Vaughan, *The Pillars of Leadership* (Nashville, TN: Highland Books, 2000).

Gregory Wilbur, *Glory and Honor: The Music and Artistic Legacy of Johann Sebastian Bach* (Nashville, TN: Cumberland House, 2005).

About the Authors

Ken Blanchard

"Suited Up" with a Passion for Leading Like Jesus

Few people have impacted the day-to-day management of people and companies more than Ken Blanchard. A prominent author, speaker and business consultant, Ken is universally characterized by friends, colleagues and clients as one of the most insightful, powerful and compassionate men in business today. Ken speaks from the heart with warmth and humor and is a polished storyteller with a knack for making the seemingly complex easy to understand.

For nearly four decades Ken Blanchard has been recognized and read as a premier thinker and writer on leadership. The three-dozen or so books (including *The One Minute Manager, Raving Fans and Gung Ho!*) he has authored or co-authored find places of prominence on bookshelves and bestseller lists here and abroad. He is a coveted and celebrated guest in national media and in major conferences and conventions. Many of the most significant national and international corporations engage Ken Blanchard for strategic counsel at the most critical levels.

Since coming to a personal faith in Jesus Christ—"suiting up," as he terms it—Ken Blanchard's passion and priority has become inspiring and equipping people to lead like Jesus. Ken has come to recognize and lift up Jesus as the greatest leadership role model of all time. Along with Phil Hodges, his friend of many years, he founded The Center for Faithwalk Leadership in 1999, now better known as Lead Like Jesus. The mission of this ministry is not to run ministries or businesses or to start churches. It has one mission: To inspire and equip the leaders who do so that, God is glorified, people are served, and organizations are more effective in impacting the world for the Kingdom of

God. Out of this small, not-for-profit organization, a movement—Lead Like Jesus—came to life with Ken as its chief champion. Visit their website at www.LeadLikeJesus.com.

A Cornell University graduate with a PhD, he has been a college professor, an entrepreneur, and business guru. He is an avid golfer and a friend to anyone who crosses his busy path! Ken and his wife Margie call California home where he is the co-founder and Chief Spiritual Officer of the Ken Blanchard Companies—a global leader in workplace learning, employee productivity, leadership and team effectiveness.

Charlie "Tremendous" Jones

Founder of Executive Books

Charlie "Tremendous" Jones, founder and president of Executive Books in Mechanicsburg, Pennsylvania, entered the gates of Heaven on October 16, 2008. He made his mark as a publisher, best-selling author and nationally acclaimed motivational speaker who also gained a reputation as an inspirational humorist and book evangelist. Mr. "Tremendous" often said, "You are today what you'll be five years from now except for the people you meet and the books you read."

At age 22 Charlie Jones entered the insurance business with MONY, and by the time he was 37 years old he helped the organization to reach over $100 million in force. He then founded Life Management Services to share his experience through seminars and consulting services.

In 2009, Executive Books became Tremendous Life Books, a dynamic publisher and wholesaler of Christian, business, and leadership materials. The bookstore is located at 206 West Allen Street in Mechanicsburg, and across the lot the company also has a 10,000-square-foot warehouse with more than one million dollars of inventory that includes books, tapes, CDs and more. Customers from all over the world go to www.TremendousLifeBooks.com to order titles distributed by Executive Books related to business, self-help, biography, and relationships, and motivational- and faith-related themes.

For more than fifty years Charlie "Tremendous" Jones' passion has been exciting people to read, think and share. In 2002 he received a Doctor of Humane Letters degree from Central Pennsylvania College, and in 2003 their new library was named the Charles "T" Jones Leadership Library in recognition of his love for reading and sharing great books.

Bob Phillips

Humorist and Author

BBob Phillips, Ph.D. is a licensed marriage and family counselor. He is the author of over 120 books with combined sales exceeding ten million books in print. He is also a New York Times Best Selling author of the Babylon Rising Series. Bob serves as the Executive Director of Hume Lake Christian Camps—one of America's largest youth camping ministries. Bob is the co-founder of the Pointman Leadership Institute. The Institute presents seminars on ethics in leadership to parliaments, government leaders, military officers, police officials, business leaders, educators, and various church leaders. The Institute has presented character-based leadership principles in 55 countries world-wide. Bob is a popular speaker and lives in California. He has two daughters and three grandsons.

The Lead Like Jesus Ministry

All people, old and young, in all cultures, in every church, in every business, in every country, and in every home desire to have leaders who model integrity, love, grace, forgiveness, and truth. We believe Jesus is the perfect role model for all leaders. Lead Like Jesus exists to help all people learn and model the leadership principles that Jesus lived.

Co-founded by Ken Blanchard, co-author of *The One Minute Manager, Lead Like Jesus: Lessons from the Greatest Leadership Role Model of All Time* and over 40 other books on leadership and management and his longtime friend, Phil Hodges, with over 35 years of experience in corporate America, Lead Like Jesus provides leadership training, resources, events, and services.

The Mission of *Lead Like Jesus*

To glorify God by inspiring and equipping people to Lead Like Jesus.

The Values of *Lead like Jesus*

- Glorify God in all we do
- Honor Jesus as the greatest leadership role model of all time
- Build relationships based on trust and respect
- Create Biblically-sound content and teaching
- Practice wise stewardship of time, talent, treasure, and influence

The *Lead Like Jesus* Picture of the Future

6.8 billion souls served daily by the impact of people leading like Jesus.

The *Lead Like Jesus* Brand Promise

The leadership model that transforms you and those you influence

To accomplish this, we envision...

- Jesus being adopted as the role model for all leaders
- People being drawn to Jesus by the impact of people leading like Jesus

The Center for Faithwalk Leadership, Inc., DBA Lead Like Jesus, is a ministry recognized as tax-exempt under Internal Revenue Code section 501(c)(3).

For more information, go to www.LeadLikeJesus.com

About Tremendous Life Books

In 2009, Executive Books became Tremendous Life Books, a fitting tribute to the memory of our founder and past president Charlie "Tremendous" Jones. Founded in 1965, Executive Books was created to share Charlie's love of books with the thousands of people who were inspired by his legendary motivational seminars.

In 2008, Charlie's mantle of leadership and enthusiasm was passed on to his daughter and friend, Tracey Jones. With a love of books and an appreciation for how they can transform lives, Tracey, along with the entire Tremendous Life staff, continues Charlie's mission, spirit and unwavering dedication to customers.

Located in Mechanicsburg, Pennsylvania, Tremendous Life Books contains a showroom where folks can browse their favorite selections and an on-site warehouse where we ship thousands of books and other media around the world. Tremendous Life Books is also a publisher dedicated to helping authors continue their mission in print.

Tremendous Life Books also supports the Books for Tremendous Living Foundation, a fund established by Charlie "Tremendous" Jones to benefit a range of organizations dedicated to developing the leaders of tomorrow.

The largest niche market wholesaler of motivational, leadership, self-help and Christian materials, Tremendous Life Books knows you'll be the same person you are five years from now except for two things: the people you meet and the books you read. To that end, our mission statement is to cultivate a love of books so that everyone can have a tremendous professional, personal, and spiritual life.

Visit Tremendous Life Books at
www.TremendousLifeBooks.com